Gooseberry Patch

Autumn

with Family & Friends

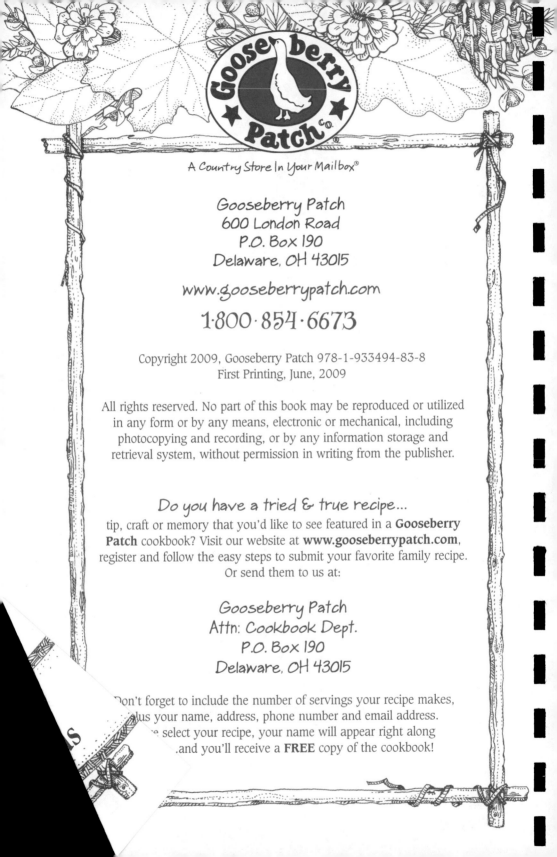

A Country Store In Your Mailbox®

Gooseberry Patch
600 London Road
P.O. Box 190
Delaware, OH 43015

www.gooseberrypatch.com

1·800·854·6673

Copyright 2009, Gooseberry Patch 978-1-933494-83-8
First Printing, June, 2009

Do you have a tried & true recipe...

tip, craft or memory that you'd like to see featured in a **Gooseberry
Patch** cookbook? Visit our website at **www.gooseberrypatch.com**,
register and follow the easy steps to submit your favorite family recipe.
Or send them to us at:

Gooseberry Patch
Attn: Cookbook Dept.
P.O. Box 190
Delaware, OH 43015

Don't forget to include the number of servings your recipe makes,
plus your name, address, phone number and email address.
If we select your recipe, your name will appear right along
...and you'll receive a **FREE** copy of the cookbook!

Contents

A Bushel of Memories 5

Come On Over! 19

A Country-Style Brunch 47

Chilly-Day Soup Suppers 71

Quick & Easy Comfort Foods 103

A Bountiful Family Feast 133

Favorite Fall Desserts 167

Treats & Sweets to Share 193

Dedicated to those who love crisp, sunny days, cool, starry nights and sharing a hayride with friends.

Dedication & Appreciation

To our family & friends...thank you for sharing your most scrumptious fall recipes.

A
Bushel
of

Memories

An Autumn Treasure Hunt

Kelly Wade
Pittsfield, IL

One of my favorite fall memories took place about 3 years ago, when my teenage daughters requested my husband, sister-in-law and I put together an Autumn Treasure Hunt. We worked diligently creating clues that would send two separate teams, consisting of a good balance of teens and adults, to various places in our rural community. The clues consisted of everything from crossword puzzles and riddles to stepping off a certain number of paces to a specific location. Everyone started at the same spot, but we sent them in opposite directions so they would not run into each other along the way. Upon arriving at the location the clue led them to, they would then find a clue marked for Team A or B that would lead them to the next location. The last clue led everyone to a lakeside location for a wiener roast and treasure that was "buried" near the campsite. Fittingly, it was a box filled with ingredients for s'mores! The first team to arrive was the "winner"...but of course, we all won, because we had a great time enjoying each other's company and the crisp autumn evening by the campfire.

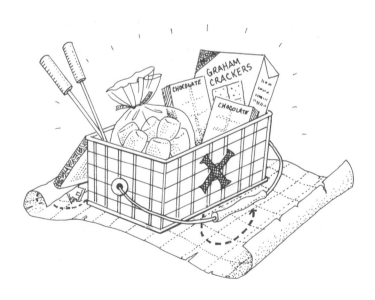

A Walk in the Woods

LeAnna Sisco
Miller, MO

Here in southwest Missouri, it is absolutely beautiful in the fall. Every year since I was very little, as soon as the leaves start turning their gorgeous autumn colors and the air starts getting a little crisp, my dad has taken me for long walks through the country woods. We just take our time to sightsee, talk and laugh! We see some critters, and always seem to see something new and amazing. I used to come home with pockets full of unique rocks and leaves and nuts, and sometimes a turtle or frog. We would spend hours out exploring and just spending precious time with each other. We have done this every year for as long as I can remember. Now that I am a grown woman with a 4-year-old son of my own, the three of us go for the same walk every year. I am so lucky that Dad loves the outdoors, takes the time to make such wonderful memories with his daughter and is now passing the same memories on to his grandson. These are memories that will last a lifetime.

7

Columbus Day Family Gathering

Mary Torrance
Henderson, NV

Every fall, all of our family members, including aunts, uncles, cousins and grandparents, gather at Letchworth State Park in western New York on the Sunday of Columbus Day weekend. This date accommodates the college kids returning for the first long weekend and usually coincides with peak leaf viewing in the area. Each family brings a homemade pot of soup or chili to keep warm on the fire and share with one & all, along with coffee, cider and various fall snacks. (Can't forget Aunt Shari's cookies!) We all go on nature trail walks, collect acorns, pine cones and leaves, play touch football and enjoy the beautiful fall foliage, the gorgeous views of the gorge, not to mention the smell of a wood-burning fire and the crispness of the leaves in the air! When we leave, it seems that we all end up at one of the local cider mills for fresh fry cakes, cider, pumpkins and apple pie! We've gone to this gathering since I was a young child and I have taken my own kids since they were young. I can smell the fall air even as I sit in my new home in Nevada!

A Bushel of Memories

Apple Picking with Grandpa

Sarah Klauss
Wadsworth, OH

Every autumn, my grandfather would take my brother, sister and me to a local apple orchard. We would each loop a basket over one arm and run around picking apples and enjoying the afternoon. The best ones were always up higher than we could reach and we would point them out for Grandpa to get for us. Afterwards, we'd come back home and help Mom make her famous chunky applesauce. Grandpa would hang out at the kitchen table drinking coffee and playing board games with us while it cooked. As soon as it was done, Mom would spoon up a big steamy bowlful sprinkled with cinnamon-sugar for each of us. Every year we'd declare that it was the best batch ever!

A Bountiful Harvest

Diane Matzdorf
Plymouth, WI

Being raised on a country farm, I recall the countless hours our family of Mom, Dad, my two sisters and I spent hours in the garden working together. My sisters and I would pick and clean piles of green and yellow beans, beets, peas and corn to be canned or frozen. I always felt secure for the winter when I walked into the fruit cellar and saw onions tied with string hanging from the ceiling, bushels of apples, pears and potatoes, crocks of carrots buried in sand, pails of ground cherries, tomatoes wrapped in tissue, and shelves and shelves of shining glass jars displaying pickles, beets, peaches, jams and jellies. That's a feeling I will always treasure.

Putting Up for Winter

Gloria Huse
Simpsonville, SC

Whenever the weather starts turning cooler, my mind goes back to my childhood days. I was raised on a small farm with my grandparents living next door to us. We always had a huge garden and worked it all summer long. When cool air hit, we got busy. Daddy and Papa would go into the woods and start chopping down trees for firewood. My job was to bring in 20 pieces of wood every evening and stack it in the basement. Grandma would start putting up all the extra garden goodies so we didn't lose a thing. We spent all our evenings rocking on the front porch shelling, shucking, snapping and peeling to prepare our wonderful bounty for the winter months. All the while, we would be laughing and talking about our day. I can still taste all those wonderful vegetables, cooked with love...and for dessert, homemade fried apple pies! Yum yum! Precious memories...life is too fast nowadays.

October Bonfire Party

Roberta Hoch
Harrisburg, PA

My husband and I started this tradition. We raised our three children in the country and every year on the first Saturday in October, rain or shine, we held a bonfire. We provided the grilled sausage, baked potatoes and warmed May wine, while our guests brought covered dishes to share with everyone. The number of guests increased every year...the first year we had 17 people and the last year we had about 150! Our children are all grown now, but they still remember these bonfires with fondness.

A Bushel of Memories

A Pumpkin Party on the Farm

Lynne Doughan
Wesley, IA

Fall and Halloween have always been my favorite times to decorate inside and out! I would spend DAYS decorating the outside of our home just for those little beggars on All Hallows' Eve. But after living in town for 18 years, we decided to move out to the farm. I thought, who's going to care what I do out here? But since Halloween is such a huge part of who I am, I invited family & friends out to carve and decorate their own pumpkins. We had some pumpkins weighing in at 100 pounds! I had paints and glitter just for the smaller children too. We had such an arrangement of pumpkins, all lined up in a row, ready to be lit for Halloween! Then we went on a hayride all around the farm, had a bonfire, cooked brats and hot dogs and served up s'mores. It was one of those beautiful fall days to be remembered as we celebrated our first Halloween here on the farm.

11

Little Princesses

Robin Muer
Encino, CA

My father, who was a Holocaust survivor from Poland, never knew what Halloween was until he came to America in 1949 at age 42. On Halloween, he always came home early from his little shoe repair shop to take my twin sister, Debbie, and me trick-or-treating. He had as much fun as we did! In 1958, when we were 7, we were princesses. Daddy made us each a beautiful powder blue satin cape with gold stars on it. Mother, who stayed home to give out candy, warned Daddy not to take us anywhere "upstairs" so we wouldn't trip over the long capes. Of course he didn't listen to her! To this day, I remember how, trying to hold onto my mask, cape and bag of candy, I went tumbling all the way down the longest staircase I ever saw. I didn't hurt myself...I was too worried about all of my candy falling out of my bag! That's one Halloween I'll never forget.

A Bushel of Memories

Colored Leaves in the Windows

Sherri Fry
Alliance, NE

I have a favorite fall memory from when I was a little girl. My family lived in a big old Victorian home built in 1904 and it had lots of huge windows. My sisters and I would gather beautiful Nebraska fall leaves and place them on wax paper, then we would shave crayons around them in contrasting colors and add another piece of wax paper on top. Then, using a hot iron, we would bond them together. We made many to display throughout our big house in all the windows. I followed this same ritual all the years that my own son was young. Now every fall I simply must walk through the town looking for those special leaves. Even if I don't hang them in the windows, they still look beautiful on a tabletop.

Leaf-Raking Fun with Dad

Penny Hart
Clarksville, AR

One of my fondest memories of autumn started out as a disliked chore. We had a big backyard and lots of trees nearby. Come fall, the leaves did...fall, that is. And it was the job of us kids to rake up those leaves and put them in piles for Dad to burn. One time we got the leaves all raked up, then noticed one of the piles moving. Dad had crawled in and covered himself with leaves, then jumped out at us! Needless to say, he soon had a pile of kids on top of him. This was followed by lots of fun and laughter, and lots more raking, of course. That night we had a big fire to burn all the leaves. As the fire burned down to hot coals, we roasted hot dogs on sticks we had picked from the woods. And for dessert, we roasted marshmallows. One of the best meals ever...at least from a kid's viewpoint!

13

Hometown Halloween Parade

Sheila Peregrin
Lancaster, PA

I grew up in a small town and every Halloween there was a parade. The high school, VFW and town bands were there, as were the town's fire trucks, the ambulance and colorful floats done by scout troops, churches and other groups. But my favorite part of the parade was the people in costumes division, because my younger brother and I always entered and usually won! My mother loved to sew Halloween costumes for us. One year we won as a Pilgrim couple; another year we won as Raggedy Ann & Andy, complete with wonderful red yarn hair. Dinner on parade night was always quick, hot and filling, something like chili that we could just grab a bowl of while Mom finished hemming or adding a final detail to our costumes. Then we got dressed and ran through town to get to the beginning of the parade. But my favorite part of the night was when the parade marched past our house. Mom would be standing on the sidewalk beaming as we walked past. Win or lose, I always felt so special seeing her waving to us as we headed towards the grandstands for the judging. Her smiles made me warm even on the chilliest nights!

A Bushel of Memories

A Family Scarecrow Party

Lea Blakney
Scotts Hill, TN

One of my favorite autumn memories and tradition is our family's annual Scarecrow Party held on our small farm in West Tennessee. During the year, we collect all the fixins'... old clothes, hats and trinkets. After an afternoon of cider and hayrides, each individual family creates their very own scarecrow and we display them as a family of scarecrows for the season. Such fun! We end the evening with a campfire and lots of treats. It could not be a more beautiful day together.

Grandma's Popcorn Balls

Donna Goodman
Delhi, LA

My favorite fall memory happened each year at Halloween. I grew up on a family farm and my grandmother's house was only a quick walk across the field. She and I would spend all day making popcorn balls for the trick-or-treaters that would be coming to her door that evening. Once the task, which was more fun than work, was completed, I would return home to dress up in my costume for the night's exciting event. We walked to Grandmother's house by the light of the moon. There has never been a more beautiful memory than the brilliance of a full moon shining down on the freshly harvested field of soybeans. When I rang the doorbell at Grandmother's house, she always acted so surprised to see me, as if I hadn't been there all day, and I acted so surprised to receive a popcorn ball from her. It was a wonderful time of pretending for young and old.

Gathering Hickory Nuts

Jennie Wiseman
Coshocton, OH

When I was young, my parents and I would go for long drives in the country. As soon as my dad saw a hickory tree, we would stop and pick up as many nuts as possible to deposit in a peck basket that we had brought along. Back home, we cracked them open and placed the nutmeats into jars to store in the freezer. We would send some to my aunt who loved them also. Then Mom would bake my dad a hickory nut cake, his favorite from when he was quite young. I savor those memories since my parents are long gone.

Trick-or-Treat!

MariBeth Parks
Andover, MN

When I was a child, there were several other children in our neighborhood in a range of ages, from three years to high school age. The older children always helped out and included the younger children in play. On Halloween night, all the children dressed up in costumes and went together from house to house trick-or-treating. We never rang a doorbell. Instead, there would be a three count, then all the children gathered on the doorstep (pushing and shoving and stepping on each other's feet) and would shout as loudly as we could, "Trick-or-treat, money or eats!" We would continue to shout until someone answered the door. This was done at each house. I still can't believe that we never lost our voices! It is a memory that is relived every Halloween at the sound of the doorbell ringing.

A Bushel of Memories

Thanksgiving Memories

Michelle Corriveau
Blackstone, MA

I remember going to my grandparents' house for Thanksgiving every year. We would sit down at a beautifully set table and feast on food prepared by Mom, the aunts, and of course, my Mémère. After dinner we would all get together and clear and clean the dishes. I remember the anticipation I felt as we were cleaning, because after it was done we would all go for a long walk in the field next door and gather creeping jenny vines to make our Christmas wreaths. Then we would go back to the house for dessert. I still remember it like it was yesterday...I am so thankful for memories like these.

Apple Pies by the Dozen

Amy Bell
Arlington, TN

When I was in college, each fall I would get together with my two best friends to make apple pies. We would drive through upstate New York where the trees were at their peak foliage, to an apple orchard. The crisp air, the smell of the apples and a cup of hot cider in our hands all set the stage for the perfect day of apple picking and pie baking. We would pick a couple of bushels of apples, and head back to one of our houses where we would bake 40 pies! Barbara would always make the crusts, while Mary and I would prepare the apple filling and the topping. There were so many laughs...like the time one of the pies got dropped upside-down in the oven! The next day, we'd hand out the pies to our delighted families, church friends and neighbors. We always had such a wonderful time that we could not wait to do it again the next year!

17

A Farmhouse Thanksgiving

Beth Schlieper
Lakewood, CO

I have wonderful memories of Thanksgiving from when I was growing up. We always went to Grammy & Pappy's house in Nazareth, Pennsylvania. On that side of the family there were seven children, plus my cousins and the great-aunts and uncles. There were always at least 40 or so people at the old farmhouse. My cousins and I would have a great time with each other playing around the farm, finding treasures in the barn and hiding up in Grammy & Pappy's bedroom! When it came time for eating...and of course the kids had to eat in the attached garage kept warm with space heaters...the meal would not be a holiday meal without Pappy's famous stuffing. He was always swatting someone's hand out of it as it cooked. Finally, after everything was cleaned up, it was time for dessert. My family just loves baking and dessert...no matter if you brought anything else along with you, you always brought dessert! What a feast for young eyes to behold! Crumb cake, lemon meringue pie, eclair cake, pumpkin pie, apple pie, cakes with cherry toppings and puddings, cookies...so many choices, or you could sample all of them, which was always my favorite option!

Come On Over!

Pepperoni Pizza Dip

Kristine Coburn
Dansville, NY

Simple to make in a slow cooker...simply delicious!

14-oz. jar pizza sauce
1 c. turkey pepperoni, chopped
8 green onions, chopped
1/2 c. red pepper, chopped
2-1/4 oz. can sliced black olives,
  drained

1 c. shredded mozzarella cheese
8-oz. pkg. cream cheese,
  softened and cubed
broccoli flowerets, cherry
  tomatoes, carrot sticks

Mix pizza sauce, pepperoni, onions, red pepper and olives in a
1-1/2 quart slow cooker. Cover and cook on low setting for 3 to
4 hours, or until heated through. Add cheeses and stir until melted.
Serve with vegetables for dipping. Makes 14 servings.

Savor a crisp, clear day by enjoying a leaf walk with your
family. See who can find the most different kinds of
fallen leaves...the biggest, the smallest, the most
brightly colored and the most unusual. Back home,
treat everyone to mugs of hot cider...what fun!

Pizza Nibblers

Jennifer Martineau
Gooseberry Patch

These little nuggets are wonderful and just a little different! I got this recipe from my mom, who persuaded a pub owner to share it with her. The pub served these yummy pretzels during their happy hour every evening.

1/2 c. oil
1 c. grated Parmesan cheese
20-oz. pkg. pretzel nuggets

1-1/4 oz. pkg. spaghetti sauce
   mix

Combine all ingredients in a large bowl; toss to coat nuggets well. Spread nuggets on a baking sheet that has been lined with aluminum foil. Bake for 45 minutes at 275 degrees. Makes 6 to 8 servings.

Look for mini enamelware pails in bright home-team colors...they're perfect for filling with crunchy party mixes!

Apple-Pecan Log

Lisa Ann Panzino DiNunzio
Vineland, NJ

A co-worker shared this recipe with me, and I have made it many times since then. This is an easy, delicious and fun appetizer to serve at a party, brunch or any special event...watch how quickly it disappears!

8-oz. pkg. cream cheese, softened
1/2 c. tart apple, cored, peeled and finely chopped
3/4 c. chopped pecans, toasted and divided

1/4 t. cinnamon
tortilla chips, snack crackers, butter cookies, apple slices, pretzels

Combine cream cheese, apple, 1/4 cup pecans and cinnamon; form into a log. Roll log in remaining pecans; cover with plastic wrap and chill for 3 to 5 hours, or overnight. Let stand at room temperature for 20 minutes before serving. Serve with a variety of dippers. Makes 6 to 8 servings.

Toasting brings out the flavor of shelled nuts.
Spread nuts in a shallow baking pan, dot with butter
and pop into a 350-degree oven. Bake for 5 to 10 minutes,
stirring occasionally and watching carefully. As soon as nuts
turn golden, remove from oven and let cool.

Berry Good Kielbasa

Rosa Smoyak
Yardville, NJ

Every year we get together with a few close neighbors for a holiday swap. This simple slow-cooker appetizer is a favorite and is always requested. It's also a big hit at football parties.

3 16-oz. pkgs. Kielbasa, sliced   32-oz. jar strawberry preserves
   into bite-size pieces

Place Kielbasa in a slow cooker and pour preserves on top, no stirring is needed. Cover and cook on low setting for 4 to 5 hours. Makes 12 to 18 servings.

Invite friends over for snacks on game day. With hearty appetizers simmering in a slow cooker or two, you'll be able to relax and enjoy the big game with your guests!

Mexican Nacho Chips

Jena Buckler
Bloomington Springs, TN

I combined two recipes to come up with this yummy appetizer, one from a friend and one from a magazine. Every time I serve it, I get rave reviews! We even enjoy the hamburger mixture as an easy meal...just spoon it over bite-size tortilla chips and garnish it with your favorite taco toppings.

2 lbs. ground beef
1 onion, finely chopped
15-oz. can black beans, drained
  and rinsed
15-oz. can corn, drained
16-oz. jar salsa

15-oz. can diced tomatoes
  with chiles
1-1/4 oz. pkg. taco seasoning
  mix
13-oz. pkg. large scoop-type
  tortilla chips

In a large skillet over medium heat, brown ground beef with onion; drain. Stir in remaining ingredients except tortilla chips. Mix well and heat through. Place a spoonful of mixture into each tortilla chip and serve immediately. Serves 10 to 12.

Hang a collection of warm fuzzy throws on wooden pegs...
ready for snuggling in nippy weather!

24

Come On Over!

Chicken Florentine Quesadillas

Wendy Ball
Battle Creek, MI

Scrapbook nights at my sister-in-law's house are always a time to relax, laugh and share stories while we scrapbook the evening away. Snacks are part of the fun too. I created this tasty appetizer by combining our favorite spinach-artichoke dip with the cheese quesadillas that I taught her son Jake how to make.

4 10-inch flour tortillas
8-oz. pkg. frozen spinach-
  artichoke dip, thawed
2 6-oz. pkgs. grilled chicken
  breast strips
1 c. shredded Mexican-blend
  cheese

1/2 red onion, thinly sliced
1/2 c. black olives, sliced
2 roma tomatoes, thinly sliced
1 green pepper, thinly sliced
Optional: sour cream, shredded
  lettuce

Warm tortillas on a griddle. Spread 2 tortillas with dip. Top with chicken strips, cheese and sliced vegetables. Add remaining tortillas; place on a lightly oiled griddle over medium-high heat. Cook for 3 to 5 minutes until heated through and cheese is melted, using a spatula to carefully turn over. Quesadillas may also be placed on a baking sheet and baked at 375 degrees for about 10 minutes. Using a pizza cutter, cut each quesadilla into 4 to 8 wedges. Garnish with sour cream and shredded lettuce, if desired. Makes 8 to 10 servings.

Celebrate Good Neighbor Day,
September 28, by
hand-delivering a cheery
potted fall mum to a neighbor.

25

Spiced Apple Tea

Jennifer Niemi
Nova Scotia, Canada

*A mug of this spicy brew really takes off the chill! Pop the spices
into a small muslin bag and you won't even need to strain it.*

5 6-inch cinnamon sticks
1 T. whole cloves
1 t. whole allspice

8 c. water, divided
1 c. instant iced tea mix
4 c. apple juice

In a small saucepan over medium heat, combine spices and 2 cups
water. Bring to a boil; reduce heat and simmer, covered, for
20 minutes. Strain, reserving liquid; discard spices. In a Dutch oven
or large saucepan, combine remaining water with tea, apple juice and
reserved liquid. Heat over low heat, stirring often, until all tea mix
has dissolved. Increase heat to medium-high; heat until piping hot.
Makes 12 servings.

A thermos filled with hot tea or coffee is a must for sipping
at hometown football games. If your thermos has been tucked
away since last autumn, freshen it up by spooning in a
heaping teaspoon of baking soda, then filling with boiling
water. Cap, shake gently and rinse...it's clean again!

Hot Cranberry Punch

Linda Thompson
Ringgold, VA

I make this every Thanksgiving and Christmas for family gatherings and church socials...it is always a hit! To keep the punch warm for the whole party, I like to just leave the pot simmering on the stove, but you could also serve it from a slow cooker.

64-oz. bottle cranberry juice
　　cocktail
12-oz. can frozen orange juice
　　concentrate
12-oz. can frozen pineapple
　　juice concentrate

3 c. water
1 t. cinnamon
Garnish: orange slices,
　　cinnamon sticks

In a 5-quart saucepan, combine cranberry juice, frozen juice concentrates, water and cinnamon. Simmer over medium-low heat, stirring occasionally until frozen juice melts and is well blended. At serving time, carefully float orange slices and cinnamon sticks on top of punch. Makes 12 to 14 servings.

A fun icebreaker for a large gathering of all ages! Divide into two teams...the goal is to line up alphabetically by everyone's first names. After 60 seconds, blow a whistle and have each team sound off by name. The team with the most participants in alphabetical order wins!

Too-Good-to-Stop Spread

Denise Reich
Acampo, CA

*This blend of creamy cheeses and savory flavors is just delicious.
Once your guests have tasted it, they won't leave the appetizer
table until it's all gone!*

8-oz. pkg. cream cheese,
   softened
8-oz. pkg. crumbled feta cheese,
   softened
2 T. balsamic vinegar
1/2 c. kalamata olives in oil,
   drained and coarsely chopped

1/2 c. sun-dried tomatoes in oil,
   drained, coarsely chopped
   and 1 T. oil reserved
10 fresh basil leaves, thinly
   sliced and divided
garlic toast, bruschetta slices or
   flavored crackers

Blend cheeses together in a medium bowl; add vinegar. Stir in olives,
tomatoes, reserved oil from tomatoes and half the basil. Line a small
bowl with plastic wrap; sprinkle with remaining basil. Pack cheese
mixture into prepared bowl. Cover with more plastic wrap and
refrigerate for an hour. At serving time, remove top piece of plastic
wrap. Invert bowl onto a serving plate and peel off remaining plastic
wrap. Serve with small slices of garlic toast, bruschetta or flavored
crackers. Serves 8 to 10.

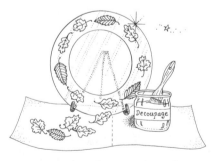

Make a pretty serving platter for cheese and other
finger foods. Brush découpage medium onto faux silk
autumn leaves and arrange them on the underside
of a clear glass plate.

Cheddar Cheese Crispies

Lorrie Smith
Drummonds, TN

A quick & easy snack! For a spicier flavor, add a little more cayenne pepper, a little black pepper and a dash of dry mustard.

8-oz. pkg. shredded sharp
   Cheddar cheese
1 c. butter, softened

2 c. all-purpose flour
1/4 t. cayenne pepper
2 c. crispy rice cereal

Combine cheese and butter; mix well. Let stand for a few minutes to soften. Add remaining ingredients; mix well. Shape into about 2 dozen balls and flatten slightly to about 1/4 to 1/2-inch thick. Place on ungreased baking sheets. Bake at 350 degrees for 15 minutes. Makes about 2 dozen.

Before the first frost, save garden cuttings to brighten a sunny windowsill. Clip stems of impatiens or coleus, pull off most of the leaves and slip them into water-filled Mason jars. When roots form, plant the cuttings in potting soil and grow indoors until spring returns.

Yummy Campfire Cheese

April Jacobs
Loveland, CO

Warm, melting cheese...a scrumptious taste treat to try at your next cookout! Or prepare this dish indoors by placing the aluminum foil packet on a baking sheet. Bake at 450 degrees for about 10 minutes.

8-oz. pkg. round Brie cheese   1 loaf crusty bread, torn
1 T. brandy or white grape juice

Set cheese in the center of a 12-inch piece of heavy-duty aluminum foil. Pierce top of cheese several times with a fork; sprinkle with brandy or juice. Seal foil tightly over cheese. Place foil packet on hot campfire coals. Cook, turning occasionally with tongs, for about 10 to 12 minutes, until cheese is soft and melted. Set packet on a heat-proof plate; open carefully. Serve with chunks of bread for scooping out warm cheese. Makes 4 to 6 servings.

With cozy fall fires beckoning, boxes of extra-long wooden matches are a useful gift. Dress up plain boxes in a jiffy with scrapbooking paper and tie on a pine cone or two with jute. Keep some on hand for spur-of-the-moment guests.

Come On Over!

Boo's Pimento Cheese

Abby Kramer
Asheville, NC

My grandfather is known as Boo. He is now 80 years old and still makes this dip to bring along whenever he comes to visit. It's the best pimento cheese I've ever tasted, and it's versatile too! It can be warmed and served as a hot cheese dip with tortilla chips or dolloped onto grilled steaks. We even like to make grilled pimento cheese sandwiches with it. Try it...you'll love it too!

3/4 lb. extra-sharp New York
    Cheddar cheese
1 lb. Colby or Longhorn cheese

2-oz. jar diced pimentos,
    drained
assorted crackers

Put cheeses into a food processor. Process until cheese starts to clump, stopping before a smooth texture is reached. Transfer cheese mixture to a large bowl and stir in pimentos. Serve with crackers. Makes 6 servings.

Score a touchdown with football-shaped dipping chips!
Use a cookie cutter to cut shapes from corn tortillas.
Spritz with non-stick vegetable spray, place on a baking
sheet and sprinkle with salt. Bake at 350 degrees
until crisp, 5 to 10 minutes.

Crispy Potato-Bacon Puffs

Becky Drees
Pittsfield, MA

*These cheesy treats are irresistible! If you're short on time, pick up
a package of ready-to-use precooked bacon.*

10 slices bacon, halved
   lengthwise

5 slices American cheese
20 frozen potato puffs

In a skillet over medium-high heat, cook bacon until partially done
but not crisp; drain. Cut each cheese slice into 4 strips. Wrap a strip
of cheese, then a bacon slice around each potato puff. Secure with a
wooden toothpick; arrange on an ungreased baking sheet. Bake at
425 degrees for 15 to 20 minutes, until bacon is crisp and potato
puffs are hot. Serve with Mustard Dipping Sauce. Serves 6 to 8.

Mustard Dipping Sauce:

1/2 c. mustard
1/4 c. brown sugar, packed

1/2 t. ground ginger
onion salt to taste

Mix ingredients well. Serve at room temperature or slightly warmed.

Do you love tailgating but can't score tickets to the big
stadium football game? Tailgating at the local Friday-night
high school game can be just as much fun...round up the
gang, pack a picnic and cheer on your team!

Beth's Party Piggies

Beth Bundy
Long Prairie, MN

With just 5 ingredients, you can stir up a party in no time at all. The plum jelly makes these little sausages unusually good.

1 c. catsup
1 c. plum jelly
4 T. mustard

1 T. lemon juice
16-oz. pkg. mini smoked
  sausages

In a saucepan over medium-low heat, combine all ingredients except sausages. Mix well. Add sausages and simmer for 10 minutes. Serve hot. Makes 40 to 50.

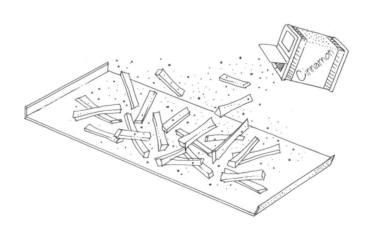

Homemade sweet potato chips...yummy! Peel sweet potatoes and slice thinly, toss with oil and spread on a baking sheet. Place on the center oven rack and bake at 400 degrees for 22 to 25 minutes, turning once. Sprinkle with cinnamon-sugar and serve warm.

Pepperoni Pinwheels

Tammy Kirby
Evington, VA

*I absolutely love **Gooseberry Patch** cookbooks and own every single one...I even have a separate bookshelf just for them! So I'm delighted to share this recipe with other readers...it always brings compliments when I serve it.*

2 8-oz. pkgs. cream cheese, softened
1-oz. pkg ranch salad dressing mix
8-oz. pkg. shredded Cheddar cheese
1/2 lb. pepperoni, diced
Optional: 2-1/4 oz. can chopped black olives, drained
Optional: 1 green pepper, diced
8 to 10 10-inch flour tortillas

Combine all ingredients except tortillas. Spread a thin, even layer of mixture onto each tortilla. Roll up tortillas and wrap; chill. At serving time, trim ends off rolls; slice into 1/4-inch pieces. Makes 50 to 60 pieces.

October gave a party,
The leaves by hundreds came...
The Chestnuts, Oaks and Maples,
And leaves of every name.

-George Cooper

Mini Veggie Pizzas

Marian Buckley
Fontana, CA

*Use whatever veggies you like! Fresh green broccoli, carrots, red onion,
yellow squash and red bell peppers look beautiful and taste great with
the mixture of three different cheeses.*

1-1/4 c. favorite vegetables,
   finely chopped
1/4 c. chopped black olives
1/4 t. lemon zest
salt and pepper to taste
5 6-inch flatbreads or pita
   rounds

4-oz. container spreadable garlic
   & herb cheese
1 c. shredded Cheddar cheese
1/4 c. Muenster cheese,
   shredded

Toss together chopped vegetables, olives, lemon zest, salt and pepper;
set aside. Spread each flatbread or pita with spreadable cheese; top
with vegetable mixture and shredded cheeses. Cut into wedges. Serve
immediately, or wrap with plastic wrap and refrigerate. Makes 12 to
15 servings.

Are you hosting a party? Take a stroll through your
neighborhood dollar store, where all kinds of colorful,
clever items for table decorating, serving and party favors
can be found...big fun at a small price!

The Dip Lady's Famous Dip

Sherry Hill
Sylacauga, AL

*No matter what the occasion, I am always asked to bring this appetizer,
a warm bread bowl filled with creamy dip. I just love knowing how
much everyone enjoys the dip made by the Dip Lady...that's me!*

1 round loaf Hawaiian-style
   bread
8-oz. pkg. cream cheese,
   softened
2-1/2 oz. pkg. deli-style sliced
   ham, chopped
8-oz. pkg. shredded sharp
   Cheddar cheese

1-1/2 c. sour cream
8-oz. pkg. shredded mild
   Cheddar cheese
1 bunch green onions, chopped
1/8 t. garlic powder
1/8 t. flavor enhancer
scoop-type corn chips

Cut a large hole in the top of bread, reserving top for a lid. Scoop
out the insides to make a bread bowl; set aside loaf. Mix remaining
ingredients except corn chips in a separate bowl until well blended.
Fill bread bowl with mixture; replace top and wrap in aluminum foil.
Bake at 350 degrees for one hour. Remove top and stir; serve with
corn chips. Serves 8 to 10.

Pick up a basket of hardy pansies
to plant in autumn. Available
in many cheerful colors, they'll
brighten the garden as it's
winding down, then will bloom
again in springtime.

Mari's Special Salsa

Mari Bochenek
Lacey, WA

I adapted this salsa from a friend's recipe and now everyone insists that I bring it to any function. It's easy, adaptable to different levels of heat, and is especially good after a day in the refrigerator. Serve it with tortilla chips or use it to sauce up some boneless chicken breasts.

2 14-1/2 oz. cans stewed
   tomatoes
4-oz. can chopped green chiles
3.8-oz. can chopped black
   olives, drained
1-1/4 c. hot salsa
1 green pepper, finely chopped

1 red pepper, finely chopped
1 bunch green onions, very
   thinly sliced
1 T. olive oil
1 T. red wine vinegar
1/8 t. salt
1/8 t. pepper

Combine both cans of tomatoes and their juice in a large serving bowl; chop up tomatoes with kitchen shears. Add chiles, olives, salsa, peppers and onions. Drizzle oil and vinegar into bowl; add salt and pepper to taste. Stir all ingredients together. Refrigerate for a few hours before serving to blend flavors. May be kept refrigerated up to 4 days. Makes about 7 cups.

Warming beverages are a must at any autumn get-together!
Whip up some name tags to slip onto mug handles. Stamp
or write names on metal-rimmed round paper tags. Slide
onto precut loops of memory wire along with a decorative
charm. A craft store will have all the supplies you need.

Zesty Pretzel Dip

Shirley McGlin
Black Creek, WI

Pretzels make a party...and this dip makes pretzels even tastier!

2 8-oz. pkgs. cream cheese,
  softened
1-oz. pkg. ranch salad dressing
  mix
16-oz. container sour cream

1 c. mayonnaise
1 c. shredded Cheddar cheese
3/4 c. beer or milk
pretzel twists or sticks

Mix together all ingredients except pretzels. Refrigerate for a few hours to allow flavors to blend. Serve with pretzels. Makes 10 to 12 servings.

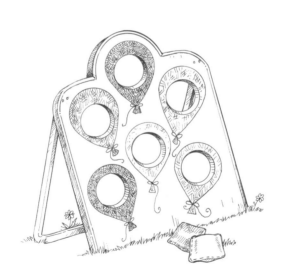

Indian Summer is perfect for a neighborhood block party... the weather is still warm and fall foliage is gorgeous. Set up tables with hay bales to sit on. Everyone can snack on favorite finger foods while waiting for burgers and hot dogs to grill. Don't forget a game of beanbag toss for the kids!

Come On Over!

Charlie's Chicken-Chive Dip

Janice Tarter
Morrow, OH

Charlie has been a life-long friend since our youthful days of working together at a fast-food restaurant. He has come to several of my parties and can always be counted on to bring this terrific dip.

8-oz. pkg. cream cheese,
   softened
2 4-1/4 oz. cans chicken spread
1 T. mayonnaise
3 T. fresh chives, chopped

1 t. soy sauce
1/4 t. celery salt
1/4 t. salt
Garnish: sesame seed, toasted
assorted crackers

Mix together all ingredients except sesame seed and crackers. Form into a ball; wrap and chill until firm. At serving time, sprinkle ball with sesame seed. Serve with crackers. Makes 20 servings.

A sunny autumn day is perfect for a family adventure. Pack the cooler with yummy snacks, load up the mini van or car and head out for somewhere you've always wanted to go... a state park, an outdoor museum or a shopping area. New memories in the making!

Creamy Cocoa 3 Ways

Linda Robson
Boston, MA

*When the weather turns damp and chilly, I like to have sweet
hot cocoa ready and waiting in the slow cooker when the kids arrive
home from school. This recipe makes it so easy, even on the busiest day!*

3/4 c. sugar
1/2 c. baking cocoa
2 qts. milk

1 T. vanilla extract
Garnish: marshmallows or
  whipped cream

Combine sugar and cocoa in a slow cooker; stir in milk. Cover and
cook on low setting for 3 to 4 hours. At serving time, stir in vanilla.
With a whisk or a hand mixer, carefully beat until frothy. Ladle hot
cocoa into mugs. Garnish with marshmallows or whipped cream.
Makes 8 to 10 servings.

Nice & Spicy Cocoa:

Add one teaspoon cinnamon and 1/8 teaspoon nutmeg along with the
cocoa. Cover and cook as directed.

Mocha Cocoa:

Prepare recipe as directed. At serving time, stir 3/4 teaspoon instant
coffee granules into each mug of hot cocoa; stir to mix.

After hydrangeas have finished blooming in late summer,
be sure to save the blossoms for year 'round decorating.
It's oh-so easy...just cut the stem of each large blossom and
tuck them into a vase. The flowers will air-dry naturally.

Hot Vanilla

Michael Curry
Ardmore, OK

This is a soothing hot drink I enjoy at night to help me sleep...I love it! With no caffeine and a delicious vanilla flavor, it's great anytime. I use fat-free milk, sugar substitute and low-fat whipped topping because of my diet, but if calories are no concern, treat yourself to whole milk and real sugar.

1 c. milk
1 T. sugar or calorie-free
  sweetener

1 t. vanilla extract
Garnish: whipped topping
Optional: candy sprinkles

Pour milk into a microwave-safe coffee mug; stir in sugar or sweetener and vanilla. Heat in microwave for about 2 minutes, until heated through. Garnish with topping and sprinkles, if desired. Serve immediately. Makes one serving.

Host a canning party! Whether you stir up one big kettle of apple butter together or make several flavors of easy freezer jams, you'll all have sweet souvenirs to take home. Be sure to have lots of vanilla wafers, round buttery crackers and cream cheese for sampling!

Antipasto Crescent Bites

Karen Boehme
Greensburg, PA

*My cousin made these for a holiday party several years ago and I have
been making them ever since for gatherings, picnics and sporting events.*

2 8-oz. tubes refrigerated
  crescent rolls
1/4 lb. deli salami, thinly sliced
1/4 lb. deli ham, thinly sliced
1/4 lb. sandwich pepperoni,
  thinly sliced
1/4 lb. provolone cheese, thinly
  sliced

1/4 lb. Swiss cheese, thinly
  sliced
12-oz. jar roasted red peppers,
  drained
3 eggs, beaten
3 T. grated Parmesan or Romano
  cheese

Arrange one tube of rolls in the bottom of a 13"x9" baking pan that has
been sprayed with non-stick vegetable spray. Pinch seams together.
Layer sliced meats and cheeses in order listed. Arrange peppers over
top layer, tearing them to make them fit. Whisk eggs and grated
cheese together; spoon half of mixture over peppers. Arrange second
tube of rolls on top, pinching seams together. Spoon remaining egg
mixture over top. Cover; bake at 350 degrees for 30 minutes. Uncover
and bake for an additional 15 minutes, until golden. Cool; cut into
bite-size pieces. Makes about 40.

Create a sweet back-to-school display on the mantel with
children's alphabet blocks, slate chalkboards, old-fashioned
school books and vintage tin lunch pails. Don't forget
a shiny apple for the teacher!

Crabmeat-Stuffed Eggs

Marilyn Miller
Fort Washington, PA

*Who doesn't love deviled eggs? This recipe is from my friend Gail.
They are delicious served as appetizers or along with the main course
at a picnic lunch.*

1 doz. eggs, hard-boiled and
  peeled
1 c. crabmeat, flaked
1 c. celery, finely chopped

2 T. green pepper, finely chopped
1 T. mayonnaise-type salad
  dressing
1/3 c. sour cream

Slice eggs in half lengthwise; remove egg yolks and mash them. Place
egg whites on a serving dish and set aside. Combine mashed yolks
and remaining ingredients; blend well. Spoon mixture into egg whites.
Chill until serving time. Makes 2 dozen.

Greet visitors with a charming homespun wreath on the
door. Simply tear checked homespun fabric in golds and
browns into strips and tie onto a grapevine wreath.

Spicy Chili Crackers

Gloria Robertson
Midland, TX

*These savory crackers are irresistible! Serve with a bowl of soup
or add to your game-day buffet table.*

16-oz. pkg. saltine crackers
1 c. olive oil
1-oz. pkg. ranch salad dressing
   mix

2 t. chili seasoning mix
1 t. garlic powder
Optional: cayenne pepper to
   taste

Place crackers in a large bowl; set aside. Combine remaining
ingredients in a separate bowl and stir to mix. Pour over crackers in
bowl; gently stir around and let stand overnight. May also be spread
on a baking sheet and baked at 250 degrees for 20 to 30 minutes.
Store in an airtight container. Makes 15 to 18 servings.

Nothing says "autumn" like a warming mug of spiced
apple cider! Pour 2 quarts of cider into a saucepan and
stir in 1/2 cup of red cinnamon candies. Simmer over
low heat, stirring constantly, until hot and candies are
dissolved, about 8 minutes.

44

Snackin' Seeds

Gladys Kielar
Perrysburg, OH

Tasty for eating out-of-hand...try sprinkling them on an autumn salad of apples and greens too.

1/2 c. pumpkin seeds	1/8 t. garlic powder
1/2 c. sunflower seeds	1/8 t. soy sauce
1 T. Worcestershire sauce	

Combine all ingredients in a small bowl; toss to mix well. Pour into a skillet over medium heat. Cook and stir for 5 minutes, until light golden. Spread on paper towels to cool. Store in a covered container. Makes one cup.

Host an old-fashioned game night. All you need are a stack of favorite board games and some yummy snacks. Pick up some whimsical prizes from a nearby dollar store...guests of all ages will have fun!

Cadillac Cocoa

Narita Roady
Pryor, OK

When our girls were younger, we lived in a small farmhouse with only one wall heater and the wind blew through the cracks. We were always looking for tasty, warm drinks yet we didn't have a lot of money. One night we put our heads together, rummaged through the cabinets and came up with this recipe...it became a family favorite!

1 env. instant hot chocolate
   mix
1 T. powdered non-dairy
   creamer

1/2 to 1 t. instant coffee
   granules
1 t. vanilla extract
1 T. marshmallow creme

Stir hot chocolate mix, creamer and coffee granules together in a mug. Add hot water as hot chocolate package instructs; stir well. Add vanilla and stir again. Top with a dollop of marshmallow creme. Makes one serving.

Share the warmth. With winter on the way, autumn is
a perfect time to pull outgrown coats, hats and mittens
out of closets and donate them to a local charity.

A Country-Style

Brunch

Apple-Cinnamon Pancakes

Staci Meyers
Montezuma, GA

Extra-special pancakes for a cool autumn morning.

4 c. biscuit baking mix
1 t. cinnamon
2 eggs, beaten

2-2/3 c. milk
1-1/2 c. apples, cored, peeled
   and chopped

Combine all ingredients; mix well. Pour by 1/4 cupfuls onto a griddle sprayed with non-stick vegetable spray. Cook over medium-low heat until bubbles appear; flip and cook the other side until golden. Serve with warm Apple Cider Syrup. Serves 4 to 6.

Apple Cider Syrup:

1/2 c. sugar
2 T. cornstarch
1/4 t. cinnamon
1/4 t. nutmeg

2 c. apple cider
2 T. lemon juice
4 T. butter

Combine sugar, cornstarch and spices in a medium saucepan over medium heat. Gradually whisk in cider and lemon juice. Bring to a boil; whisk for one minute and remove from heat. Add butter, whisking until melted and well blended.

Dried apple slices make a folky garland. Slice apples thinly, soak in lemon juice for 20 minutes and pat dry. Spread slices on a baking sheet and bake at 200 degrees for 2 to 3 hours. String slices on jute and hang across a mantel, window or doorway...they'll smell delicious!

A Country-Style Brunch

Sweet & Spicy Bacon

Zoe Bennett
Columbia, SC

Try this easy-to-fix bacon at your next brunch...guests will love it!

1/2 c. brown sugar, packed
2 T. chili powder
1 t. ground cumin
1 t. cumin seed

1 t. ground coriander
1/4 t. cayenne pepper
10 thick slices bacon

Line a 15"x10" jelly-roll pan with aluminum foil. Place a wire rack on pan and set aside. Combine all ingredients except bacon; sprinkle mixture onto a large piece of wax paper. Press bacon into mixture, turning to coat well. Arrange in a single layer on prepared pan; place pan on center rack of oven. Bake at 400 degrees for 12 minutes; turn bacon over. Bake for an additional 10 minutes, until deep brown but not burned. Drain on paper towels; serve warm. Serves 4 to 5.

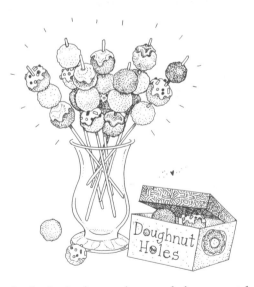

Doughnut hole kabobs...what a delicious idea! Slide bite-size doughnut holes onto wooden skewers and stand the skewers in a tall vase for easy serving.

49

New England Cider Doughnuts

Regina Vining
Warwick, RI

The perfect partner for a cup of tangy warm cider.

1 c. apple cider	2 t. baking powder
1 c. sugar	1 t. baking soda
1/4 c. shortening	1/2 t. cinnamon
2 eggs, beaten	1/2 t. salt
1/2 c. buttermilk	1/4 t. nutmeg
3-1/2 c. all-purpose flour	oil for deep-frying

Boil cider in a small saucepan over medium heat until it is reduced to 1/4 cup, 8 to 10 minutes; let cool. Beat sugar with shortening until smooth. Add eggs and mix well; add buttermilk and reduced cider. In a separate bowl, stir together remaining ingredients except oil. Add to cider mixture; stir just enough to combine. Pat out dough 1/2-inch thick on a lightly floured surface. Cut dough with a 2-3/4" doughnut cutter, reserving doughnut holes. Fill a large saucepan with 3 inches of oil; heat to 375 degrees. Fry several doughnuts at a time until golden, turning once or twice, about 4 minutes. Remove to paper towels with a slotted spoon. Cook doughnut holes for one to 2 minutes. Drizzle with Cider Glaze; serve warm. Makes 1-1/2 dozen.

Cider Glaze:

2 c. powdered sugar	1/4 c. apple cider

Stir together sugar and cider to a glaze consistency.

Serve hot spiced coffee with sweet autumn treats. Simply add 3/4 teaspoon pumpkin pie spice to 1/2 cup ground coffee and brew as usual.

50

A Country-Style Brunch

Cranberry Crescent Rolls

Janice Knutson
Sparta, WI

*These rolls are delicious...good enough to serve at our bed & breakfast.
Even better, they're really easy to make.*

8-oz. tube refrigerated crescent
   rolls
1 c. cranberries, chopped

1 T. sugar
Optional: 1 c. powdered sugar,
   1 to 2 T. milk

Unroll crescent rolls; place on a greased baking sheet. Mix together cranberries and sugar; spoon evenly onto crescent rolls. Roll up crescents. Bake at 375 degrees for 11 to 13 minutes, until lightly golden. If desired, mix together powdered sugar and enough milk to make a drizzling consistency. Drizzle over baked rolls. Serve warm or cool. Makes 8.

Choose the prettiest leaves to preserve for crafting
and decorating. Arrange leaves in a flat pan and cover
with a mixture of one part glycerin and two parts water.
Use a rock to keep the leaves submerged for one week,
then remove and blot dry with paper towels...they'll
retain their brilliant colors all season long.

Garlic Mushrooms on Toast

JoAnn

An elegant light breakfast dish...good made with plain button mushrooms or a mixture of portabella and cremini mushrooms. If you have a secret place to hunt morel mushrooms, they would be yummy in this recipe.

2 slices bacon, chopped
1-1/2 lbs. mushrooms, stemmed
   and sliced
2 cloves garlic, minced
1/2 t. dried rosemary
1/4 t. salt

pepper to taste
Optional: 1/4 c. white wine
4 to 6 slices bread, toasted,
   buttered and halved
   diagonally

In a skillet over medium heat, cook bacon until partially done but not crisp. Add mushrooms, garlic and seasonings. Cook, stirring occasionally, for 8 to 10 minutes, until most of the liquid has evaporated. Pour in wine, if using; cook and stir for an additional minute. Spoon mushroom mixture over toast triangles. Makes 4 to 6 servings.

For a hearty brunch buffet dish, serve fluffy scrambled eggs
in baked potato boats. Bake potatoes the night before,
then halve and scoop out, reserving the potato shells.
To serve, reheat shells in a 400-degree oven for about
15 minutes while the eggs are cooking. Spoon eggs into
"boats" and garnish as desired.

A Country-Style Brunch

Chicken & Waffles

Virginia Watson
Scranton, PA

Such a funny combination...but it's really tasty, so give it a try!

3 lbs. chicken
salt and pepper to taste
2 to 4 T. olive oil
2 14-1/2 oz. cans chicken broth
1 stalk celery, chopped

1 carrot, chopped
1 onion, chopped
1 bay leaf
3 T. all-purpose flour
1/4 c. cold water

Sprinkle chicken with salt and pepper. Heat oil in a large deep skillet over medium-high heat. Add chicken to skillet; cook on all sides until golden. Add broth, vegetables and bay leaf to skillet. Reduce heat to low; cover and simmer until chicken is tender, about one hour. Remove chicken, reserving broth in skillet. Cool chicken and tear into bite-size pieces. Discard vegetables. Skim fat from reserved broth; bring broth to a boil. Shake together flour and water in a small jar until smooth. Add flour mixture gradually to skillet, stirring constantly. Continue to cook until gravy is thickened. Return chicken to skillet; keep warm over low heat. Serve chicken and gravy over waffles. Serves 4.

Golden Waffles:

2 c. biscuit baking mix
1-1/3 c. milk
1 egg, beaten

2 T. oil
Optional: 1/2 t. poultry
    seasoning

Stir together all ingredients until blended. Pour batter by 1/2 cupfuls onto a preheated, lightly greased waffle iron. Bake waffles according to manufacturer's directions.

For lighter-than-air waffles,
simply use club soda
instead of milk or water.

Cranberry-Pumpkin Loaf

Lori Knowles
El Cajon, CA

About 25 years ago, I came up with this recipe. I didn't have enough cranberries on hand, so I substituted a can of cranberry sauce. The result was delicious and I've been making it ever since...people go absolutely bananas over this bread! It freezes really well too.

2 c. sugar
2 eggs, beaten
1/2 c. oil
1 c. canned pumpkin
16-oz. can whole-berry
  cranberry sauce

2-1/4 c. all-purpose flour
1/2 t. salt
1 t. baking soda
1 T. pumpkin pie spice
1 c. chopped pecans

Blend together sugar, eggs, oil, pumpkin and cranberry sauce in a large bowl; set aside. In a separate bowl, mix flour, salt, baking soda and spice. Add flour mixture to pumpkin mixture, a little at a time; stir until well mixed. Stir in pecans. Spread batter into 2 lightly greased and floured 9"x5" loaf pans. Bake at 325 degrees for 45 to 55 minutes, until a toothpick inserted in the center comes out clean. Makes 2 loaves.

For a festive gift, wrap a folded tea towel around a plastic-wrapped loaf of nut bread and tie it with a large ribbon. Hot-glue a silk flower onto the ribbon.

Bountiful Bread

Denise Webb
Galveston, IN

This recipe is jam-packed with yummy stuff like maraschino cherries, pecans, raisins and coconut. It makes four of the cutest little loaves, baked in empty fruit cans...perfect for gift giving to lucky friends!

3 eggs, beaten
1/2 c. oil
1/2 c. milk
2-1/2 c. all-purpose flour
1 c. sugar
1 t. baking powder
1 t. baking soda
1 t. cinnamon
1/2 t. salt

2 c. carrots, peeled and
 shredded
1-1/3 c. sweetened flaked
 coconut
1/2 c. maraschino cherries,
 chopped
1/2 c. raisins
1/2 c. chopped pecans

Whisk together eggs, oil and milk; set aside. In a separate bowl, sift together flour, sugar, baking powder, baking soda, cinnamon and salt. Add egg mixture; mix just until well combined. Stir in remaining ingredients. Spoon batter into 4 empty, clean 16-ounce fruit or vegetable cans that have been well greased and floured. Set cans on a baking sheet. Bake at 350 degrees for 45 to 50 minutes. Turn out of cans onto wire racks; cool thoroughly. Wrap loaves in plastic wrap; refrigerate overnight. Makes 4 mini loaves.

Tuck a crock of maple butter into a basket alongside a loaf of fresh-baked bread...what a scrumptious way to tell a friend, "I'm thinking of you." Blend 2 tablespoons maple syrup and a teaspoon of pumpkin pie spice into a stick of softened butter.

Garden Quiche

Sharon Tillman
Hampton, VA

This yummy stovetop quiche is a clever way to use up odds & ends of fresh veggies and cheese from the fridge...feel free to substitute what you have on hand! Sometimes we enjoy it with a cup of tomato soup as a pleasant light lunch.

1 T. butter
1/4 c. onion, finely chopped
2 T. green or red pepper,
   chopped
1 clove garlic, minced
1/2 lb. yellow squash, thinly
   sliced
1/2 lb. broccoli flowerets,
   coarsely chopped

2 eggs, beaten
1/4 c. milk
1/8 t. cayenne pepper
1/4 t. dry mustard
1/4 t. dried marjoram
1/2 c. shredded Swiss cheese
2 T. grated Parmesan cheese

Melt butter in a skillet over medium heat. Add onion and green or red pepper; sauté until soft and golden. Stir in garlic, squash and broccoli; cover and cook for 3 to 5 minutes, just until tender. Whisk together eggs, milk and seasonings; stir in Swiss cheese. Pour mixture over vegetables in skillet; sprinkle with Parmesan cheese. Reduce heat to low. Cover and cook for 5 minutes, or just until eggs are set and cheese has melted. Cut into wedges to serve. Makes 2 to 4 servings.

Spice up breakfast with some cider-glazed sausages. Brown and drain a 1/2-pound package of breakfast sausage links. Add a cup of apple cider to the skillet, then turn heat down to low and simmer for 10 minutes. Yummy!

A Country-Style Brunch

Baked Egg Soufflé

Lynne McKaige
Savage, MN

Easy and delicious...I hope you'll enjoy this dish as much as we do!

12 slices white bread
2 T. butter, softened
6 slices deli ham
6 slices American cheese

3 c. milk
4 eggs, beaten
salt and pepper to taste

Spread one side of each bread slice with butter. Arrange 6 slices butter-side down in a lightly buttered 13"x9" baking pan. Arrange ham and cheese on top. Cover with remaining bread, butter-side up. Whisk milk and eggs together until frothy; pour over all. Sprinkle with salt and pepper. Bake, uncovered, at 350 degrees for 50 minutes, or until golden. Let stand for 5 minutes before serving. Serves 6.

Mom's Special French Toast

Stacey Keef
Walnut Hill, IL

This recipe was handed down from my mom, who was known by family & friends for her wonderful home cooking. Mom always made this for special breakfasts and brunch gatherings.

2 T. corn syrup
1/2 c. margarine
1 c. brown sugar, packed
1 loaf French bread, sliced
   1-inch thick

5 eggs, beaten
1-1/2 c. milk
1 t. vanilla extract
1/4 t. salt
Garnish: powdered sugar

In a small saucepan over low heat, simmer corn syrup, margarine and brown sugar for several minutes. Pour into a greased 13"x9" baking pan. Arrange bread in pan over syrup mixture. Whisk together eggs, milk, vanilla and salt; pour over bread. Cover and refrigerate overnight. Cover and bake at 350 degrees for 30 to 40 minutes. Sprinkle with powdered sugar. Serve warm. Makes 8 to 10 servings.

All-in-One Breakfast Bake

Beth Bundy
Long Prairie, MN

*This is a great make-ahead recipe! You'll love to wake up knowing
there's a wonderful breakfast in the fridge, just waiting to be popped
into the oven. Your guests will be even happier when they taste it.*

1 loaf English muffin toasting
　bread, crusts trimmed
2 to 3 T. butter, softened
1 c. shredded Cheddar cheese
1 c. shredded mozzarella cheese
10 slices cooked ham or
　Canadian bacon
8 eggs, beaten

3 c. milk
1/2 t. dry mustard
1/2 t. salt
1 c. assorted vegetables like
　mushrooms, tomatoes
　and green or red peppers,
　chopped
3 T. butter, melted

Spread one side of each bread slice with butter. Place half the slices
butter-side up in the bottom of a lightly buttered 13"x9" baking pan.
Layer with cheeses, ham or bacon and remaining bread slices,
butter-side up. Beat together eggs, milk, mustard and salt; pour over
top. Cover and refrigerate overnight. Before baking, sprinkle with
chopped vegetables; drizzle with melted butter. Bake, uncovered,
at 350 degrees for one hour. Makes 15 servings.

Invite your best girlfriends over for brunch! Share goodies,
small talk and a quick craft to double as a party favor...
lavender sachets to tuck into sweater drawers. Fill muslin
drawstring bags with dried lavender, then enclose each bag
in a vintage flowered hankie and tie with a pretty ribbon.

Cheddar-Chile Brunch Potatoes

Kathy Arner
Phoenix, AZ

This recipe came to me years ago from the school where I work...it is requested every time we have a staff breakfast. It's easy to make and can be made the night before. I have served it at church brunches too and there's never any leftovers. My family pouts when they know the whole pan goes with me, so I have to make two pans!

1-lb. pkg. ground pork sausage, browned and drained
16-oz. container light sour cream
10-3/4 oz. can cream of chicken soup
7-oz. can diced mild green chiles

8-oz. pkg. shredded Cheddar cheese
30-oz. pkg. frozen shredded hashbrowns, thawed
30-oz. pkg. frozen spicy or western shredded hashbrowns, thawed

Mix all ingredients except hashbrowns in a large bowl; stir until well mixed. Add hashbrowns and stir until coated well. Transfer to a greased 15"x11" baking pan. Bake, uncovered, at 375 degrees for one hour, or until deep golden. Let stand for 5 minutes before serving. Makes 12 servings.

Cabin-shaped maple syrup tins make whimsical candleholders for the breakfast table. Tuck tapers into the opening and arrange in a group.

Marsha's Breakfast Delight Scones
Marsha Nichols
El Reno, OK

These scones really are a treat when spread with a little butter...
they're even good plain. I like to cut them out with a
heart-shaped cookie cutter.

2 c. lowfat biscuit baking mix
1/2 c. plus 2 T. sugar
2 T. semi-sweet chocolate chips,
   coarsely chopped
1/4 c. sweetened dried
   cranberries, chopped

1 T. orange zest
2 T. orange juice
1 t. vanilla extract
1/2 c. skim milk
Garnish: 1 to 2 T. melted butter,
   1 to 2 T. sugar

Combine biscuit mix, sugar, chocolate chips, cranberries and orange zest. Mix orange juice and vanilla in a separate bowl; add to flour mixture. Stir in milk a little at a time, just until moistened. Turn out dough onto a lightly floured surface. Shape into an 8-inch circle and cut into wedges, or cut with desired 2-inch cookie cutters. Place on greased baking sheets. Brush tops of scones with melted butter; sprinkle with sugar. Bake at 450 degrees for about 10 minutes; do not overbake. Makes 6 to 8.

Warm baked apples are yummy for brunch. Spoon mincemeat pie filling into the center of cored Rome Beauty or Granny Smith apples and place in a casserole dish. Bake at 350 degrees until soft, about 45 to 60 minutes.

A Country-Style Brunch

Chocolate Chip-Pumpkin Muffins
Sheri Graham
Moundridge, KS

We LOVE these muffins! They are so moist...they are my kids' most-requested breakfast. I like to use silicone muffin pans. They don't need to be greased at all and the muffins pop right out.

3 c. whole-wheat flour
1 c. buttermilk
1 c. honey
1/2 c. butter, melted
4 eggs, beaten
15-oz. can pumpkin

2 t. baking powder
2 t. baking soda
1 t. cinnamon
1 t. salt
12-oz. pkg. semi-sweet
   chocolate chips

The night before, mix flour, buttermilk, honey and melted butter in a non-metallic bowl; cover with plastic wrap. Let stand on the counter overnight. In the morning, add eggs and pumpkin; beat with an electric mixer on medium speed until smooth. Beat in baking powder, baking soda, cinnamon and salt. Stir in chocolate chips by hand. Spoon batter into greased muffin cups, filling 2/3 full. Bake at 400 degrees for 18 to 20 minutes. Makes about 2 dozen.

Dress up a pumpkin in a brand-new way...glue on bright-colored leaves in a pattern with tacky glue. Snip the edges of the leaves to make them lay flat.

Make-Ahead Sausage Brunch Bake

Vickie

Send this recipe south of the border! Make it with Mexican-blend cheese, spicy sausage and a generous spoonful or two of salsa.

10 slices bread, crusts trimmed
1 doz. eggs
3 c. milk
2 t. dry mustard

8-oz. pkg. shredded Cheddar
   cheese
1 lb. ground pork sausage,
   browned and drained

Arrange bread slices in a lightly greased 3-quart casserole dish; set aside. Whisk together eggs, milk and mustard; stir in cheese and sausage. Pour mixture over bread; cover and refrigerate overnight. In the morning, bake, uncovered, at 350 degrees for one hour, until set. Serves 8 to 10.

Kathy's Bacon Popovers

Kathy Grashoff
Fort Wayne, IN

Mmm...bacon! An easy tote-along breakfast to enjoy.

2 eggs
1 c. milk
1 T. oil
1 c. all-purpose flour

1/4 t. salt
3 slices bacon, crisply cooked
   and crumbled

Whisk together eggs, milk and oil. Beat in flour and salt just until smooth. Fill 12 greased and floured muffin cups 2/3 full with batter. Sprinkle bacon over batter. Bake at 400 degrees for 25 to 30 minutes, or until puffed and golden. Serve warm. Makes one dozen.

Hashbrown Breakfast Pizza

Traci Green
Orange Park, FL

Let the kids help put together this fun breakfast dish...they'll love eating their creation.

8-oz. tube refrigerated crescent rolls
1 lb. ground pork sausage, browned and drained
1 c. shredded Cheddar cheese
2 T. grated Parmesan cheese

1 c. frozen shredded hashbrowns, thawed
5 eggs, beaten
1/4 c. milk
1/2 t. salt
1/8 t. pepper

Separate rolls and press together to form a crust on an ungreased 12" pizza pan. Layer with sausage, cheeses and hashbrowns; set aside. Whisk eggs, milk, salt and pepper together and pour over hashbrowns. Bake at 375 degrees for 30 minutes. Cut into wedges. Serves 6.

There are so many fun harvest festivals, antique sales and county fairs every autumn...be sure to visit at least one! A hearty breakfast together with family & friends will start the day off right.

Sausage & Jack Pie

Ursula Juarez-Wall
Dumfries, VA

Here's a quick and tasty breakfast dish that will satisfy any hungry family...my four girls make short work of it!

2 8-oz. tubes refrigerated
  crescent rolls
2 8-oz. pkgs. brown & serve
  breakfast sausage links,
  browned and sliced
4 c. shredded Monterey Jack or
  Colby Jack cheese

8 eggs, beaten
1-1/2 c. milk
2 T. onion, chopped
2 T. green pepper, chopped
1/2 t. salt
1/4 t. pepper
1/4 t. dried oregano

Separate each can of crescent rolls into 2 large rectangles. Place rectangles side-by-side in an ungreased 13"x9" baking pan to form a crust, covering bottom and halfway up sides of pan. Press to seal perforations. Arrange sausages over crust; sprinkle with cheese. Combine remaining ingredients and pour over cheese. Bake, uncovered, at 400 degrees for 20 to 25 minutes. Serves 8 to 10.

If the weather report calls for frost and there are still green tomatoes in the garden, don't fret! Pick them, wrap individually in newspaper and place in a brown paper bag. In one to two weeks they'll be ripe and red.

Potato & Onion Frittata

Wendy Jacobs
Idaho Falls, ID

Make a hearty, warm breakfast using a little leftover ham and potato from last night's dinner.

2 to 3 T. olive oil, divided
1 yellow onion, peeled and
   thinly sliced
1/4 c. cooked ham, diced
1 c. potatoes, peeled, cooked
   and diced

4 eggs, beaten
1/3 c. shredded Parmesan
   cheese
salt to taste

Heat 2 tablespoons oil over medium heat in a non-stick skillet. Add onion; cook and stir for 2 to 3 minutes. Add ham and potatoes. Cook until onion and potatoes are lightly golden. With a slotted spoon, remove mixture to a bowl; cool slightly. Stir eggs, cheese and salt into onion mixture. Return skillet to medium heat; add the remaining oil, if needed. When skillet is hot, add onion mixture. Cook until frittata is golden on the bottom and top begins to set, about 4 to 5 minutes. Place a plate over skillet and carefully invert frittata onto the plate. Slide frittata back into skillet. Cook until bottom is lightly golden, 2 to 3 minutes. Cut into wedges; serve warm or at room temperature. Makes 4 servings.

Make some Halloween memories...invite friends to visit, dress up in thrift-shop costumes and take pictures, make popcorn balls together and watch all the old, classic monster movies!

Maple Cream Coffee Treat

Tonya Lewis
Scottsburg, IN

Every time my family comes to visit from out of town, I make these the first morning. Everyone loves these cream cheese-filled rolls... they're perfect with coffee.

1 c. brown sugar, packed
1/2 c. chopped pecans
1/3 c. maple-flavored syrup
1/4 c. butter, melted
8-oz. pkg. cream cheese,
  softened

1/4 c. powdered sugar
2 T. butter, softened
Optional: 1/2 c. sweetened
  flaked coconut
2 12-oz. tubes refrigerated
  flaky biscuits

In a greased 13"x9" baking pan, combine brown sugar, nuts, syrup and melted butter. Spread evenly in bottom of pan; set aside. Blend cream cheese, powdered sugar and softened butter until smooth; stir in coconut, if using, and set aside. Separate dough into 20 biscuits; press or roll each biscuit into a 4-inch circle. Spoon one tablespoon of cream cheese mixture down center of each biscuit to within 1/4 inch of edge. Overlap sides of dough over filling, forming finger-shaped rolls. Arrange rolls seam-side down over brown sugar mixture in pan in 2 rows of 10 rolls each. Bake at 350 degrees for 25 to 30 minutes, or until deep golden. Let stand for 3 to 5 minutes before inverting onto a serving platter. Serves 5 to 6.

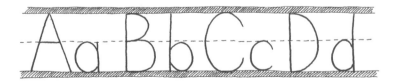

During the first week of school, deliver a tray of your favorite breakfast goodies to the teachers' lounge... it's sure to be appreciated!

A Country-Style Brunch

Caramel-Apple Bread Pudding

Lynn Williams
Muncie, IN

Spoil brunch guests with this wonderful dish that's filled with fall flavors. Add a skillet of breakfast sausages and a steamy pot of coffee or tea for a complete breakfast they'll love.

2 Granny Smith apples, cored,
   peeled and sliced
1/4 c. water
3/4 t. cinnamon
1/2 c. brown sugar, packed
2 T. light corn syrup
2 T. butter

1/4 c. chopped pecans
1 loaf Italian bread, sliced
   1/2-inch thick and divided
3 eggs, beaten
1-1/4 c. milk
1 t. vanilla extract
1/4 t. nutmeg

In a small saucepan over medium heat, cook apples in water until tender, about 7 to 10 minutes. Drain apples; toss with cinnamon and set aside. Add brown sugar, corn syrup and butter to saucepan. Cook and stir over medium heat just until mixture boils. Pour into an ungreased 2-quart casserole dish; sprinkle with pecans. Arrange 4 to 5 bread slices on top of mixture. Spoon apples evenly over bread; arrange remaining 4 to 5 bread slices on top. Whisk remaining ingredients together; pour over bread. Press bread down gently to moisten completely. Cover and refrigerate for 3 hours to overnight. Uncover; bake at 325 degrees for 40 to 45 minutes, until a knife tip inserted near center tests clean. Run knife around edges to loosen; cool in dish on a wire rack for 15 minutes. Carefully invert bread pudding onto a serving platter. Cut into triangles and serve warm, with caramel sauce from dish spooned over top. Makes 8 servings.

I have always been delighted at the prospect of a new day,
a fresh try, one more start, with perhaps a bit of magic
waiting somewhere behind the morning.

-J.B. Priestley

67

Hashbrown Brunch Bake

Ellen Folkman
Crystal Beach, FL

This tasty recipe came from my mother, Jennie Miller, about 10 years ago. I treasure all the recipes I get from my mom because she's a great cook. I make this for my family, usually for special occasions like birthdays and holidays.

1/2 lb. bacon
1/2 c. onion, chopped
1/2 c. green pepper, chopped
1 doz. eggs
1 c. milk
1 c. shredded Cheddar cheese

16-oz. pkg. frozen shredded
   hashbrowns, thawed
1 t. salt
1/2 t. pepper
1/4 t. dill weed

In a skillet over medium-high heat, cook bacon until crisp. Remove bacon, reserving drippings in skillet; crumble bacon and set aside. In reserved drippings, sauté onion and green pepper until tender; remove with a slotted spoon. Whisk eggs and milk together in a large bowl; stir in remaining ingredients along with onion mixture and bacon. Transfer to a greased 13"x9" baking pan. Bake, uncovered, at 350 degrees for 35 to 45 minutes, or until a knife inserted near center comes out clean. Makes 8 to 10 servings.

A little trick for extra-rich hot chocolate...place a pat of butter in each mug before pouring in the hot chocolate.

Smoked Salmon Strata

Mary Muchowicz
Elk Grove Village, IL

*This is a scrumptious brunch dish to share with good friends.
It's really easy too, so you'll have more time to spend visiting.*

3 to 4 onion bagels, halved
3-oz. pkg. cream cheese,
   softened
1 T. butter, softened
5-oz. pkg. smoked salmon,
   sliced
dill weed to taste

8-oz. pkg. shredded Italian-
   blend cheese, divided
1 doz. eggs, beaten
1 c. half-and-half
1/2 t. salt
1/4 t. pepper
2 T. Dijon mustard

Spread bagel halves with cream cheese; cut each half into 4 pieces.
Spread butter in a 13"x9" baking pan. Arrange bagel pieces in pan,
cream cheese side up; top each with a small piece of salmon. Sprinkle
with dill weed; sprinkle one cup shredded cheese over salmon layer.
Beat eggs, half-and-half, salt, pepper and mustard together; pour
over cheese layer. Sprinkle remaining cheese over egg mixture.
Bake, uncovered, at 350 degrees for 20 to 30 minutes. Makes
10 to 12 servings.

Mix up some autumn potpourri. Combine nature-walk
finds like seed pods and nuts with whole cloves, allspice
berries and cinnamon sticks from the kitchen spice
rack. Toss with a little cinnamon essential oil and
place in a shallow decorative bowl.

Autumn Sweet Potato Hash

Becky Drees
Pittsfield, MA

*A delightfully different side to serve with creamy scrambled eggs
and hot buttered toast.*

3 T. olive oil
2 c. sweet potatoes, peeled and
   diced
2 c. butternut squash, peeled
   and diced
1/2 c. red pepper, diced
1/2 c. green pepper, diced

1/2 c. onion, diced
1/2 t. garlic, minced
1/4 c. fresh sage, thinly sliced
1/4 t. salt
1/4 t. white pepper
1/2 c. vegetable broth

In an oven-proof sauté pan over medium heat, combine oil, sweet
potatoes, squash, peppers and onion. Sauté until vegetables begin to
soften and turn golden. Add garlic, sage, salt and pepper; continue to
sauté for one minute. Stir in broth. Bake, uncovered, at 350 degrees
just until vegetables are tender, about 10 to 15 minutes. A little more
broth may be added to keep hash from drying out. Serves 6 to 8.

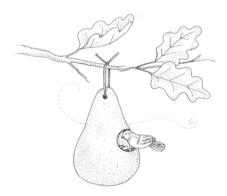

Make gourd bird feeders for feathered friends to enjoy all
winter long. Cut a large opening in a bottle gourd with a
craft knife, then drill a hanging hole in the top and a
drainage hole in the bottom. Fill with a mix of sunflower
seeds and millet to attract a variety of birds.

Chilly-Day

Soup Suppers

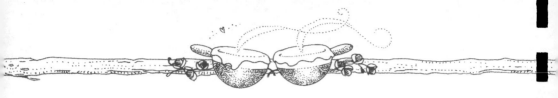

Tortellini-Sausage Soup

Nancy Willis
Farmington Hills, MI

Your family will love this hearty, savory soup. Toss a crisp green salad
and pop some garlic bread in the oven...dinner is served!

1 lb. ground Italian pork
   sausage
1 c. onion, chopped
2 cloves garlic, minced
4 c. beef broth
1/2 c. dry red wine or beef broth
28-oz. can crushed tomatoes
28-oz. can diced tomatoes

15-oz. can tomato sauce
1 c. carrots, peeled and chopped
1/2 t. dried basil
1/2 t. dried oregano
1 T. dried parsley
1 c. zucchini, chopped
9-oz. pkg. refrigerated cheese
   tortellini, uncooked

Brown sausage in a large stockpot over medium heat; drain. Add
onion and garlic; sauté until tender. Stir in broth, wine or broth,
tomatoes with their juice, tomato sauce, carrots and herbs. Bring to a
boil; stir well. Reduce heat; cover and simmer for 30 minutes. Stir in
zucchini and tortellini; cover and simmer for an additional 15 minutes.
Makes 10 to 12 servings.

A yellowware bowl of shiny red apples doubles as
a casual centerpiece and as a quick, healthy snack.

Hearty Vegetable-Beef Soup   *JoAnn*

Everyone needs a great chilly-day recipe for veggie beef soup and this is mine! On busy days, I'll use a slow cooker. Combine the browned beef and onion with everything else except the peas and herbs, cover and cook on low for 8 to 10 hours. Stir in the peas and herbs half an hour before dinner is served.

1 lb. stew beef, cubed
1 onion, chopped
1 T. oil
4 c. beef broth
3 c. water
14-1/2 oz. can crushed
  tomatoes
1 c. carrots, peeled and sliced

1-1/2 c. potatoes, peeled
  and cubed
1 c. celery, sliced
1 c. green beans, sliced
1/2 c. corn
1/2 c. frozen peas
1/2 t. dried basil
1/2 t. dried oregano

In a stockpot over medium heat, cook beef and onion in oil until beef is browned. Add broth, water, tomatoes and their juice. Reduce heat and simmer until beef is nearly tender, about 1-1/2 hours. Add carrots, potatoes, celery, green beans and corn; continue to simmer another 30 minutes. Stir in frozen peas and herbs; simmer just until peas are tender. Makes 4 servings.

A soup supper in front of a crackling fire...how cozy!
Invite friends to bring their favorite veggies and cook up a
big pot of hearty vegetable soup together. While the soup
simmers, you can catch up on conversation.

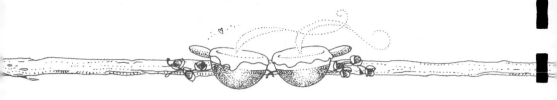

Minnesota Wild Rice Soup

Margaret Haase
Lake City, MN

This soup's flavor is even better if made a day ahead,
refrigerated overnight and reheated.

6 T. butter
1/2 c. onion, chopped
1 c. sliced mushrooms
1/2 c. all-purpose flour
3 c. chicken broth

1/2 c. wild rice, cooked
3 c. cooked ham, diced
1/2 c. carrots, peeled and grated
1/2 c. slivered almonds
1 c. half-and-half

Melt butter in a large saucepan over medium heat. Add onion and mushrooms; cook until tender. Blend in flour; gradually add broth. Cook and stir constantly until broth comes to a boil. Stir in rice, ham, carrots and almonds; simmer for 5 minutes. Add half-and-half; heat through without boiling. Makes 10 to 12 servings.

Polka-dot pumpkins! Hollow out pumpkins of two or three different colors like orange, white and green. Punch out round plugs from each pumpkin with an apple corer and just swap the plugs between pumpkins.

Slow-Simmered Split Pea Soup

*Sally Burke
Lansing, MI*

*A scrumptious use for leftover baked ham! If you have a ham bone,
add it to the pot right at the beginning for extra flavor.*

16-oz. pkg. dried split green
  peas
1/4 c. dried split yellow peas
3 qts. water
1 onion, chopped
2 T. chicken bouillon granules
1/4 to 1/2 t. pepper

1 bay leaf
3/4 lb. cooked ham, finely
  chopped
1-1/2 c. carrots, peeled and
  thinly sliced
1 c. celery, chopped
1 potato, peeled and cubed

In a large soup pot, combine dried peas, water, onion, bouillon, pepper
and bay leaf. Simmer over low heat, uncovered, for 1-1/2 to 2 hours.
Add remaining ingredients. Cook for an additional 1-1/2 to 2 hours,
stirring occasionally, until peas and vegetables are tender and desired
thickness is reached. Discard bay leaf before serving. Makes 6 servings.

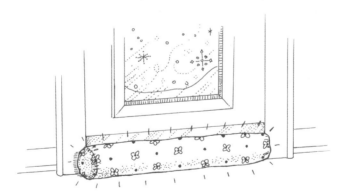

Chilly breezes are blowing! Make a door draft stopper.
Cut a 30-inch by 6-inch strip of fabric. Fold it in half
lengthwise, right sides together. Stitch down the long edge
and across one end. Turn it right-side out and fill it up
with sand. Tuck in the other end and stitch it closed.

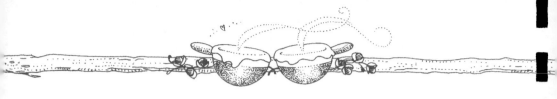

Cabbage Fruit Slaw

Suzanne Conn
Fostoria, OH

*A luscious, colorful cool-weather salad. Add some shredded carrots
along with the cabbage, if you like.*

4 c. shredded cabbage
2 oranges, peeled and cut in
   bite-size pieces
2 red apples, cored and chopped
1 c. red seedless grapes, halved

1/2 c. mayonnaise
1/4 c. milk
1 T. cider vinegar
3/4 T. honey
1/3 c. chopped pecans

In a large bowl, toss together cabbage, oranges, apples and grapes.
In a small bowl, stir together mayonnaise, milk, vinegar and honey.
Cover and refrigerate both bowls. Just before serving, stir dressing into
salad and top with pecans. Makes 4 to 6 servings.

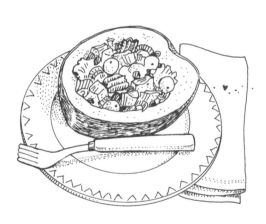

Scoop out the inside of an acorn squash and use it
as a serving bowl for creamy coleslaw or chicken salad.

Bountiful Apple Salad

Jackie Smulski
Lyons, IL

Orange zest and orange yogurt give this yummy salad an unexpected zing! Sprinkle with sugared nuts for a special touch.

1 red apple, cored and diced
1 green apple, cored and diced
1/2 c. celery, thinly sliced
1/3 c. golden raisins
1 T. orange zest
1/4 c. mayonnaise

1/4 c. orange yogurt
1 T. lemon juice
3 c. shredded lettuce
Optional: chopped walnuts
    or pecans

In a large bowl, mix apples, celery, raisins and orange zest; set aside. Mix mayonnaise, yogurt and lemon juice together in a small bowl; gently fold into apple mixture. Salad may be refrigerated for an hour, if desired. Arrange lettuce on a platter or in an oblong serving dish; spoon salad over lettuce. Garnish with chopped nuts, if desired. Makes 4 to 6 servings.

Sugared walnuts are delicious tossed over a crisp fall salad. Place 3/4 cup walnuts, 1/4 cup sugar and one teaspoon butter in a cast-iron skillet. Cook and stir over medium heat for about 7 minutes, until sugar is golden and melted. Spread carefully on a greased baking sheet and let cool completely.

77

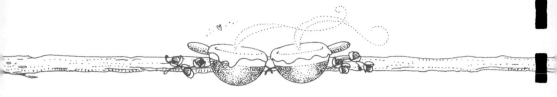

Beefy Nacho Cheese Soup

Shelly McMurtrey
Rison, AR

Stir up this hearty soup in a jiffy for your hungry family...
it has just five ingredients!

1 lb. ground beef
2 c. beef broth
8-oz. jar picante sauce
1/8 t. ground cumin
10-3/4 oz. can nacho cheese
    soup

In a large saucepan over medium heat, brown ground beef; drain. Add broth, picante sauce and cumin; bring to a boil. Reduce heat; cover and simmer for 15 minutes, stirring frequently. Stir in cheese soup; gently heat through without boiling. Serves 6.

Top your favorite spicy soup with crunchy tortilla strips.
Brush olive oil over both sides of flour tortillas.
With a pizza cutter, cut the tortillas into narrow strips.
Place strips on a baking sheet and bake at 375 degrees for
5 to 7 minutes, turning once or twice, until crisp and golden.

Lucille's Mexican Cornbread

*Nanette Jordan
Kuna, ID*

This is the most wonderful cornbread I have ever tasted! It is perfectly seasoned and not too spicy. The recipe is from a lovely lady named Lucille Renner, who is a very young 87 years old. Lucy has served this cornbread with fried catfish for as long as she can remember.

2 c. cornmeal
3/4 c. all-purpose flour
1 T. baking powder
1/2 t. baking soda
1 t. salt
14-3/4 oz. can creamed corn
1-1/4 c. sour cream or buttermilk
3/4 c. oil
3 eggs, beaten
7-oz. can chopped green chiles, drained
2 green peppers, chopped
1 jalapeño pepper, seeded and chopped
1-1/2 c. shredded Cheddar cheese, divided

In a large bowl, combine all ingredients except cheese; mix well. Pour half of batter into a greased large cast-iron skillet. Spread half of the cheese on top. Pour in remaining batter and put remaining cheese on top. Bake at 350 degrees for 35 minutes. Cut into wedges. Makes 12 servings.

Tin cans with colorful, vintage-looking labels make the best country-style vases. Tuck small bouquets of mums into several cans and line them up along a windowsill or group them on a table.

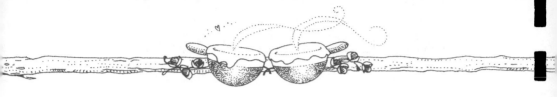

Zesty Artichoke Salad

Kathy Grashoff
Fort Wayne, IN

A fresh-tasting salad that's delicious any time of year...it's an easy make-ahead too. Make the dressing, toss together all the salad ingredients except the lettuce, and refrigerate both. At serving time, just add the lettuce and toss with the dressing...ready to serve!

1 head red leaf lettuce, torn
14-oz. can quartered artichoke
   hearts, drained
6-oz. can black olives, drained
1 red onion, thinly sliced

4 roma tomatoes, coarsely
   chopped
8-oz. pkg. shredded provolone
   cheese

Combine all ingredients in a large salad bowl; toss to mix. Drizzle with Parmesan Vinaigrette and toss gently to coat. Serve immediately. Serves 6.

Parmesan Vinaigrette:

2/3 c. oil
1/3 c. red wine vinegar
1/3 c. shredded Parmesan
   cheese
1 t. Italian seasoning

1 t. dried parsley
1/4 t. garlic powder
1/8 t. salt
1/4 t. pepper

Whisk ingredients together until blended. Use immediately or cover and refrigerate.

Top a salad with grilled apple slices...yummy with pears too!
Heat a tablespoon each of olive oil and maple syrup in
a grill pan. Add thin slices of tart apple. Cook for
6 to 8 minutes, turning once, until deep golden
and crisp. Serve warm.

Garlic Bubble Bread

Joanne Grosskopf
Lake in the Hills, IL

This is a flavorful dinner version of Monkey Bread and it is super easy to make! Whenever I serve it, someone asks for the recipe.

1-lb. loaf frozen bread dough	1 t. garlic powder
1/4 c. butter, melted	1/2 t. garlic salt
1 T. dried parsley	Optional: sesame or poppy seed

Thaw dough according to package directions; cut into one-inch pieces. In a small bowl, combine melted butter, parsley, garlic powder and garlic salt. Dip dough pieces into butter mixture to coat; layer in a buttered 9"x5" loaf pan. Sprinkle sesame or poppy seed over the top, if desired. Cover and let rise until double, about one hour. Bake at 350 degrees for about 30 minutes, until golden. Makes 4 to 6 servings.

Greet visitors with a bountiful farmstyle display on the front porch. Set a bale of hay in front of a shock of dried cornstalks, then heap the bale with brightly colored pumpkins, squash and kale. Add a pot or two of mums and you're done!

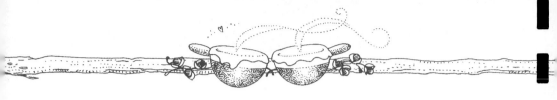

Autumn Beef Barley Soup

Cindy Amice
Mechanicsburg, PA

Teriyaki sauce is the surprise ingredient in this tasty soup.

1 lb. ground beef
1/2 c. onion, chopped
3 cloves garlic, minced
8-oz. pkg. sliced mushrooms
1/2 t. dried basil
garlic salt to taste
salt and pepper to taste
3 c. water
1 c. beef broth

1/4 c. teriyaki sauce
1 T. balsamic vinegar
1 c. carrots, peeled and chopped
1 c. potatoes, peeled and
  chopped
1/2 c. celery, chopped
16-oz. can diced tomatoes
1/2 c. catsup
1/2 c. pearled barley, uncooked

Place ground beef, onion, garlic and mushrooms in a large pot; sprinkle with seasonings. Cook over medium heat until beef is browned; drain. Add remaining ingredients except barley; bring to a boil. Stir in barley; reduce heat and simmer for 30 minutes to one hour. Makes 4 servings.

For the easiest-ever fall centerpiece, simply lay a wreath of
autumn leaves or bittersweet berries on the table and
set a pumpkin in the center...so clever!

Tom Turkey Noodle Soup

Emily Edwards
Alliance, OH

A family tradition for Thanksgiving weekend.

2 18-1/2 oz. cans turkey broth
4-2/3 c. water
1 T. dried parsley
1 t. dried, minced onion
4 c. cooked turkey, diced
8-oz. pkg. kluski egg noodles,
  uncooked

Combine broth, water, parsley and onion in a large stockpot over medium heat; bring to a boil. Add turkey and noodles; reduce heat and simmer for 10 to 15 minutes. Serves 4 to 6.

Savory smells were in the air. On the crane hung steaming kettles, and down among the red embers copper saucepans simmered, all suggestive of some approaching feast.

-Louisa May Alcott

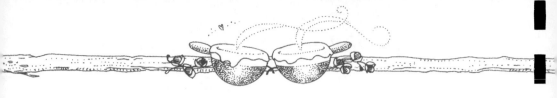

Hobo Stew

Char Pletcher
Lone Grove, OK

I always like to put on a kettle of my Hobo Stew on Halloween so my family can have something warm to eat before they head out to trick-or-treat. It's what they love the most! We eat it with crackers and cheese. The whole house smells delicious when friends drop by.

1 lb. ground beef
1 onion, diced
1 T. seasoned salt with onion
  and garlic
4 potatoes, peeled and cubed
3 carrots, peeled and sliced
28-oz. can whole tomatoes,
  broken up

15-1/4 oz. can corn
15-oz. can ranch-style beans
14-1/2 oz. can green beans
1.35-oz. pkg. onion soup mix
.87-oz. pkg. brown gravy mix
1-oz. pkg. ranch salad
  dressing mix

In a large stew pot over medium heat, brown ground beef with onion and seasoning. Drain; add remaining ingredients and enough water to cover. Bring to a boil; reduce heat. Simmer until vegetables are tender, about 30 to 40 minutes, adding a little more water if needed. Serves 8 to 10.

Start your own Halloween dinner tradition! In the morning, put on a soup pot or slow cooker of chili, beef stew or vegetable soup to simmer. It will be easy for everyone to grab a bowlful while putting on costumes or in between handing out treats.

84

The Great Pumpkin Chili

Kelly Durocher
Schenectady, NY

I won a chili contest through my local newspaper with this recipe.
The pumpkin adds great flavor and makes the chili very creamy.
My girls love this chili...I hope you enjoy it too!

3 lbs. ground beef
3 14-1/2 oz. cans diced
   tomatoes
2 15-oz. cans kidney beans,
   drained and rinsed
15-oz. can pumpkin

2 green peppers, chopped
2 onions, chopped
2 T. chili powder
2 T. honey
1/4 t. cayenne pepper
1 t. salt

Brown ground beef in a large pot over medium heat, stirring to crumble; drain. Stir in remaining ingredients; reduce heat to low. Simmer, covered, for one to 2 hours, adding water as necessary. Makes 12 servings.

Did you know a prize-winning pumpkin gains about
20 to 30 pounds a day at its peak growing time?
That's a lot of pumpkin!

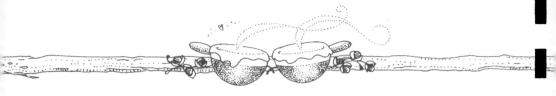

Minestrone Pasta Salad

JoAnn

A hearty salad, chock-full of veggies...yummy with crusty deli-style sandwiches. If fresh asparagus and green beans are out of season, it's fine to use canned ones...just drain, no cooking required.

16-oz. pkg. tubetti pasta,
   uncooked
1 lb. asparagus, cut into
   bite-size pieces
1/2 lb. green beans, cut into
   bite-size pieces
3/4 lb. new redskin potatoes,
   cooked and thickly sliced

15-1/2 oz. can cannellini beans,
   drained and rinsed
6-oz. jar roasted red peppers,
   drained and sliced into strips
10-oz. jar basil pesto sauce
salt and pepper to taste

Cook pasta according to package directions, adding asparagus and green beans during final 2 to 3 minutes. Drain; rinse with cold water and drain again. Place pasta mixture in a large salad bowl; add potatoes, cannellini beans and red peppers. Stir in pesto sauce to taste; add salt and pepper as needed. Chill until serving time. Serves 10 to 12.

Volunteer for a day at a local soup kitchen. Whether you're chopping veggies, stirring the kettle or serving up bowls of hot soup, your help is sure to be appreciated.

Warm Orzo Salad

Amber Goldstein
Spring, TX

I like to serve this as a side dish with chicken...it's a tasty meatless main dish too.

1 green pepper, chopped
1 yellow pepper, chopped
1 red pepper, chopped
1 onion, minced
1 T. oil
14-3/4 oz. can corn, drained

15-1/2 oz. can black beans,
   drained and rinsed
14-1/2 oz. can diced tomatoes
1/4 c. Italian salad dressing
8-oz. pkg. orzo pasta, cooked

In a large skillet over medium-low heat, cook peppers and onion in oil until tender. Add corn, beans and tomatoes with juice; mix well. Simmer, uncovered, for 15 minutes. Add salad dressing and cooked orzo to vegetables in skillet; mix well. Serve warm. Makes 4 to 6 servings.

Make autumn leaf napkin toppers...an easy craft for kids. Roll out polymer clay in colors like orange, gold, red and brown, then cut out with leaf-shaped mini cookie cutters. Cut a small hole at the top with a drinking straw and bake as package directs. Tie each leaf onto a rolled-up dinner napkin with a strand of jute.

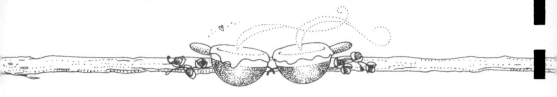

Classic French Onion Soup

Carol Donnelly
San Bernardino, CA

This delicious restaurant favorite is easy to make at home.

3 T. olive oil
3 sweet onions, thinly sliced
3 14-1/2 oz. cans beef broth
1/2 t. salt

4 thick slices French bread,
  toasted
1 c. Gruyère or Swiss cheese,
  shredded

Heat oil in a large saucepan over medium heat. Add onions and cook until lightly golden. Reduce heat; cook for 30 to 40 minutes until deep golden, stirring frequently. Add broth and salt. Reduce heat to low; simmer for 15 to 20 minutes. Ladle soup into 4 oven-proof bowls; top each bowl with a toasted bread slice and sprinkle with cheese. Broil 4 inches from heat for 2 to 3 minutes, until cheese is bubbly and lightly golden. Makes 4 servings.

Tuck a fall floral arrangement of yellow spider mums and orange gerbera daisies into a vintage soup tureen...a whimsical table decoration for a casual soup supper.

Mom's Chilly-Day Cheese Soup

Regan Reeves
Panama, IL

My mom always made this soup when the weather turned cold.
Now I make it for my family...they love it too!

8 potatoes, peeled and diced
1 onion, chopped
2 qts. water
2 16-oz. pkgs. frozen broccoli,
   cauliflower and carrot blend
10-3/4 oz. can cream of celery
   soup

10-3/4 oz. can cream of chicken
   soup
16-oz. pkg. pasteurized process
   cheese spread, cubed

Combine potatoes, onion and water in a large saucepan. Bring to a boil over medium-high heat. Reduce heat and simmer until tender, 15 to 20 minutes. Add frozen vegetables; cook until tender, about 12 to 15 minutes. Stir in soups; mix well. Add cheese and simmer for a few more minutes, until cheese is melted. Makes 4 to 6 servings.

Soup is sure to be even tastier served up in toasty bread bowls. Slice the tops off bread rounds, scoop out and spritz with non-stick olive oil spray. Sprinkle with Italian seasoning and grated Parmesan cheese, if you like. Bake for about 10 minutes at 350 degrees.

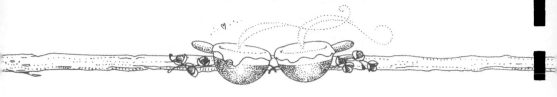

Cheesy Broccoli Soup

Pam Kittle
Clay City, IN

With all the ingredients on hand in the pantry and fridge,
this soup is quick & easy to make.

2 10-3/4 oz. cans cream of
   potato soup
10-3/4 oz. can cream of
   onion soup
3-1/2 c. milk
1/2 c. water

10-oz. pkg. frozen chopped
   broccoli, thawed
1-1/3 c. pasteurized process
   cheese spread, cubed
1/3 c. cream cheese, cubed

Combine all ingredients in a large saucepan. Cook over medium-low
heat, stirring often, until heated through and cheeses have melted.
Makes 8 to 10 servings.

Visit a pottery studio with friends and try your hand at
"throwing" soup bowls. Decorate and fire your creations
to take home...even the simplest bowls will serve up
fun memories along with the soup!

Rose's Cream of Potato Soup

Rose Cannon
Gordon, AL

Garnish this thick, cheesy soup with snipped chives.

1/2 onion, chopped
1/4 c. butter
8 potatoes, peeled and cubed
2 t. roasted garlic & red bell
  pepper seasoning blend
salt and pepper to taste

10-3/4 oz. can cream of chicken
  soup
1 c. shredded mozzarella cheese
1 c. shredded Parmesan cheese
1/2 c. Colby cheese, shredded
2 to 2-1/2 c. milk

In a large saucepan over medium heat, sauté onion in butter. Add potatoes and enough water to cover; stir in seasonings. Cook until potatoes break apart with a fork. Stir in soup; add cheeses and stir until melted. Stir in milk to desired thickness; adjust seasoning. Cook, stirring occasionally, for a few more minutes until thickened. Makes 4 to 6 servings.

November 15 is National Clean-Out-Your-Refrigerator Day...cook up a big pot of "surprise soup" with whatever you find! Raw onion, celery, carrot and green pepper should be sautéed first, then add cooked, chopped veggies and meat. Pour in broth to cover, season to taste and simmer for about 30 minutes.

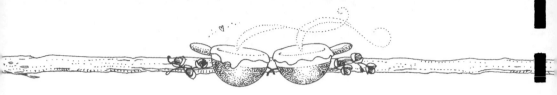

Auntie Rosie's Onion Bread

Pamela Schlimmer
San Jose, CA

My Aunt Rosie was a great cook and came up with this recipe many, many years ago. Her memory lives on every time I make this yummy bread. It's always a hit...I usually have to make two loaves!

3/4 c. butter
1.35-oz. pkg. onion soup mix

1/2 c. grated Parmesan cheese
1 loaf sourdough French bread

In a small saucepan, melt butter over low heat. Add soup mix and Parmesan cheese; stir well. Slice loaf as for garlic bread, without cutting all the way through. Spoon butter mixture evenly between slices. Place loaf on a lightly greased baking sheet. Bake at 425 degrees until golden, about 15 minutes. Serves 6.

September, October and early November are ideal for fall bulb planting. Why not get together with neighbors to plant everyone's bulbs? Afterwards, share mugs of soup and homemade bread fresh from the oven.

Broccoli Cornbread

Janet McCann
Ball, LA

I love to serve this cornbread to anyone who hasn't had the pleasure of trying it...I'm always asked for the recipe afterwards.

1/2 c. butter, melted
1/3 c. onion, chopped
1/2 t. salt
3/4 c. cottage cheese

10-oz. pkg. frozen chopped broccoli, thawed and drained
4 eggs, beaten
8-1/2 oz. pkg. corn muffin mix

In a large bowl, mix all ingredients except muffin mix. Stir in muffin mix and pour into an ungreased 13"x9" baking pan. Bake at 400 degrees for 20 to 25 minutes. After baking, place bread under the broiler briefly until golden, if desired. Cut into squares. Makes 8 servings.

Tea towels from the 1950's are perfect bread-basket liners...
they'll keep freshly baked bread toasty warm and add
a dash of color to the table.

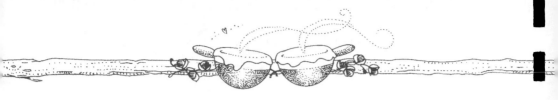

Grandma's Pear Salad

*Dana Dowell
Glendale, AZ*

When I was growing up, my grandmother would make this salad for family get-togethers. I wouldn't try it because I don't like pears very much. When I had my first baby, my family brought me dinner shortly after I was released from the hospital, and my grandma brought along her pear salad. Not wanting to hurt her feelings, I tried a spoonful... I realized that I had missed out on many years of enjoyment by not trying Grandma's Pear Salad earlier!

8-oz. pkg. cream cheese,
  softened
1 c. frozen whipped topping,
  thawed

15-1/4 oz. can pear halves,
  drained
1 c. boiling water
3-oz. pkg. lemon gelatin mix

Place cream cheese, whipped topping and pears in a blender; set aside. Pour boiling water into a small bowl; stir in gelatin until dissolved. Pour gelatin into blender with other ingredients. Blend until well mixed. Pour into an 8-cup serving bowl; refrigerate until set. Serves 6.

Picture-perfect portions of a favorite gelatin salad are handy for buffets or potlucks. Spoon the gelatin mixture into paper muffin liners and set in a baking pan. Chill until firm, then peel off liners.

Pineapple-Cranberry Salad

Eleanor Paternoster
Bridgeport, CT

*Fruity and refreshing...equally good with Thanksgiving dinner
or on a brunch buffet.*

20-oz. can crushed pineapple,
    drained and juice reserved
6-oz. pkg. raspberry gelatin mix
16-oz. can whole-berry
    cranberry sauce

1 apple, cored, peeled and
    chopped
2/3 c. chopped walnuts

Combine reserved pineapple juice with enough water to equal 3 cups;
pour into a medium saucepan. Bring to a boil over medium heat;
remove from heat. Add gelatin mix; stir for 2 minutes. Stir in
cranberry sauce. Pour into a large bowl; refrigerate for 1-1/2 hours,
or until slightly thickened. Stir in pineapple, apple and walnuts.
Return to refrigerator and chill for 4 hours, until firm. Makes
12 to 14 servings.

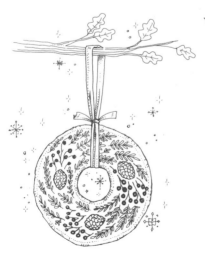

When autumn weather turns cold,
make an ice wreath to hang from
your outdoor tree branches.
Arrange greenery and some fresh
cranberries inside a round gelatin
mold, add two inches of water,
then freeze. Fill the mold
completely with water and freeze
again. Turn the wreath out of the
mold and hang from a length of
wide jute upholstery webbing.

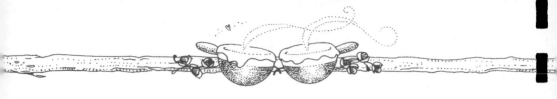

Warm German Potato Salad

Judy Loemker
Edwardsville, IL

This recipe has been passed down in my family for generations, but was never written down. My Grandma Siever just tossed things in until she had the right blend. I wanted to duplicate her recipe, so Mom helped me decide how much of each ingredient to add. One evening Grandma came for supper just as I was putting on the finishing touches. I asked her to sample my version. She took a taste and lavished praise on me... only to turn around (when she thought I wasn't looking!) and begin adding a pinch of this & a dash of that. Grandma had no idea that I was watching her "doctor up" the salad! It has been a family joke for over 40 years now.

10 lbs. redskin potatoes
1 lb. bacon, chopped
1-1/2 c. cider vinegar
1 c. water
1-1/2 c. sugar

2-1/2 t. salt
1-1/4 c. onion, finely chopped
5 eggs, hard-boiled, peeled and
  sliced
Garnish: paprika

Cover potatoes with water in a large stockpot. Boil until soft, but not falling apart. Remove potatoes with a slotted spoon as they become done; drain on paper towels. Empty stockpot and return it to stove; add bacon and fry until crisp. Remove bacon and drippings, reserving 4 tablespoons drippings in stockpot. Add vinegar, water, sugar, salt and onion to pot. Cook for 5 to 7 minutes over medium heat, stirring occasionally; remove from heat. While vinegar mixture cooks, peel and slice warm potatoes. Add potatoes to pot along with bacon and 4 sliced eggs; stir well until coated. Adjust sugar and salt to taste; spoon salad into a large serving bowl. Top with remaining sliced egg and sprinkle with paprika. Let stand before serving so potatoes can soak up sauce. Serve warm. Serves 20.

Jan's Redskin Potato Salad

Janice Myers
Mechanicsburg, PA

Perfect for an autumn bonfire picnic.

1 c. mayonnaise
1 c. sour cream
1 c. ranch salad dressing
1 stalk celery, diced
1 bunch green onions, diced
8-oz. pkg. shredded sharp
   Cheddar cheese

4 eggs, hard-boiled, peeled and
   divided
2 lbs. redskin potatoes, cooked
   and diced
Garnish: paprika

Mix mayonnaise, sour cream and salad dressing in a large bowl. Add celery, onions, cheese and 3 eggs, diced; mix well. Add potatoes; mix well again. Top with remaining egg, sliced, and sprinkle with paprika. Chill for at least 2 hours before serving. Makes 8 to 10 servings.

Throw an Oktoberfest party for family & friends. Set a festive mood with polka music. Toss some brats on the grill to serve in hard rolls...don't forget the spicy mustard! Round out the menu with potato salad, sauerkraut, homemade applesauce and German chocolate cake for dessert. Everyone is sure to have a wonderful time together!

Easy Taco Soup

Carie VanCleave
Abilene, TX

One day I was so hungry for soup. I found some canned beans, tomatoes and corn in the pantry, added a few other ingredients and made a fantastic soup...my family loves it! Garnish it with shredded cheese and crushed tortilla chips.

1 lb. ground beef
14-1/2 oz. can beef broth
16-oz. can pinto beans
16-oz. can black beans
15-1/4 oz. can corn
10-oz. can diced tomatoes
    with chiles
1 yellow squash, chopped

1 zucchini, chopped
2 c. water
1-1/4 oz. pkg. taco seasoning
    mix
1-oz. pkg. ranch salad dressing
    mix
2 T. fresh cilantro, chopped
salt and pepper to taste

In a large stockpot over medium heat, cook ground beef until browned; drain. Stir in remaining ingredients. Reduce heat and simmer until squash and zucchini are tender, about 15 minutes. Serves 8.

Watch tag sales for a big red speckle enamelware stockpot... it's just the right size for cooking up a family-size batch of soup. The red color adds a homey touch to any soup supper!

Mary's Sweet Corn Cake

Mary Murray
Gooseberry Patch

We just love scoops of this warm, yummy cornbread served alongside a bowl of chili.

1/2 c. butter, softened	3 T. yellow cornmeal
1/3 c. masa harina flour	2 T. whipping cream
1/4 c. water	1/4 t. baking powder
10-oz. pkg. frozen corn, thawed	1/4 t. salt
1/3 c. sugar	

With an electric mixer on medium speed, beat butter in a large bowl until creamy. Gradually add flour; beat in water and set aside. Place corn in a food processor or blender. Pulse to chop coarsely; stir into butter mixture. Mix remaining ingredients well; stir into butter mixture. Pour into a greased 8"x8" baking pan; cover with aluminum foil. Set in a 13"x9" baking pan; add water 1/3 of the way up around small pan. Bake at 350 degrees for 50 to 60 minutes. Uncover; let stand for 15 minutes. Scoop with a small scoop; serve warm. Serves 8.

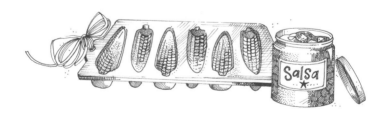

Add zest to a favorite chili or vegetable soup recipe in a jiffy! Just stir in a generous amount of spicy salsa.

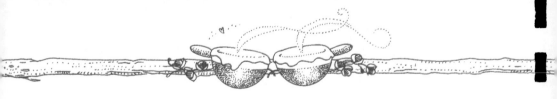

Slow-Cooker Steak Chili

Mignonne Gardner
Pleasant Grove, UT

All summer I long for cool, crisp autumn nights. I created this recipe just for those fabulous fall nights. The aroma of chili fills my home while it simmers. It makes me giddy for Halloween!

2 T. oil
2 lbs. beef round steak, cut into
   1-inch cubes
1-1/2 c. onion, chopped
2 cloves garlic, minced
1-1/3 c. water, divided
1 c. celery, chopped
2 15-oz. cans kidney beans,
   drained and rinsed
2 14-1/2 oz. cans diced
   tomatoes

16-oz. jar salsa
15-oz. can tomato sauce
1-1/2 T. chili powder
1 t. ground cumin
1 t. dried oregano
1/2 t. pepper
1/8 c. all-purpose flour
1/8 c. cornmeal
Garnish: shredded Cheddar
   cheese, sour cream, crushed
   tortilla chips

Heat oil in a large sauté pan over medium heat; add meat, onion and garlic. Cook until meat is browned and onion and garlic are translucent. With a slotted spoon, remove meat and onion to a slow cooker, leaving juices behind in pan. Add one cup water, celery, beans, tomatoes with juice, salsa, sauce and seasonings to slow cooker; stir. Cover and cook on low setting for 8 hours. Shortly before serving time, place flour, cornmeal and remaining water in a small bowl and whisk until smooth. Add mixture to simmering chili; stir for 2 minutes, until thickened. Garnish as desired. Serves 8.

Choose a crisp fall evening to host a bonfire party. Gather friends of all ages...serve chili, hot cider and s'mores, tell ghost stories and sing songs together. You'll be making memories that will last a lifetime!

Easy Chicken Noodle Soup

Melissa Harrell
Wahoo, NE

My family loves chicken noodle soup, but I don't always have time to make homemade soup from scratch, starting with making the broth. This is really easy...a great meal for a chilly autumn night!

2 14-1/2 oz. cans chicken broth
2 10-3/4 oz. cans cream of
   chicken soup
6 c. water
12-1/2 oz. can chicken, drained
2 cubes chicken bouillon
1/2 c. celery, diced

1/4 c. carrot, peeled and thinly
   sliced
1/2 to 1 t. lemon pepper,
   dill weed or seasoned salt,
   as desired
8-oz. pkg. wide egg noodles,
   uncooked

Combine broth, soup and water in a medium soup kettle; stir until well blended. Add chicken, bouillon cubes, celery, carrot and desired seasoning. Bring to a boil over medium heat, stirring occasionally. Turn down to medium-low heat; add noodles and stir. Cook for an additional 10 to 15 minutes or until noodles are tender, stirring occasionally to keep noodles from sticking. Serves 6.

Toting some homemade chicken soup to a friend who's under the weather? Remember all the nice things that go along with making someone feel better... crossword puzzles, a book by a favorite author, a box of tissues and a hot water bottle.

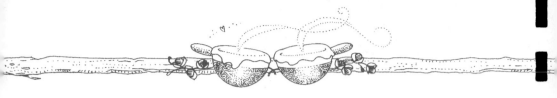

Bacon Bread

Karen Christiansen
Glenview, IL

When I was a little girl, my Lithuanian grandmother made the most delicious bacon buns. If I close my eyes, I can see myself in her kitchen, snitching tastes of the sweet dough from the old wooden bowl it was rising in. Nowadays I'm too busy to make rolls by hand, but this recipe for the bread machine comes close to that taste I love!

2 T. plus 1-1/2 t. butter, divided	1-1/4 c. warm milk,
1 onion, finely chopped	75 to 80 degrees
2 slices bacon, diced	3-1/2 c. bread flour
1/4 t. allspice	1-1/2 T. sugar
1/8 t. cinnamon	1-1/2 t. salt
1/8 t. ground cloves	1-3/4 t. active dry yeast

Melt 1-1/2 teaspoons butter in a non-stick skillet over medium heat; add onion and cook until soft. Add bacon and spices; lower heat and simmer about 5 minutes, until bacon is cooked but not crisp. Remove skillet from heat. Place remaining ingredients, including butter, into a bread machine, according to manufacturer's instructions. Set bread machine to white bread setting. If machine has a dispenser for adding ingredients mid-cycle, put the onion mixture in there. Otherwise, add it halfway through the second knead cycle. When the bread machine has finished, remove loaf from pan. Makes one loaf.

Pick up a new-to-you fall fruit like quince, persimmon or pomegranate at a farmstand. Ask the vendor how to prepare them...he or she is sure to have some tasty suggestions to share!

Quick
& Easy

Comfort Foods

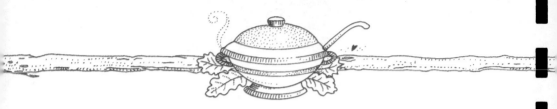

Crunchy Chicken "Toes"

Lisa Johnson
Hallsville, TX

This recipe for hot, crunchy chicken "toes" came from a friend of the family. With its special crunchy breading, it gets lots of requests from kids of all ages!

1 c. corn flake cereal, crushed
1 c. plain bread crumbs
2 T. brown sugar, packed
1 t. salt
1/2 t. pepper
1/2 t. allspice
3 T. oil

1/3 c. all-purpose flour
2 eggs, beaten
1-1/2 lbs. chicken breast
   tenders, cut into 2-inch
   pieces
1/4 c. honey mustard
1/4 c. barbecue sauce

Mix together crushed cereal, bread crumbs, sugar and seasonings in a shallow bowl. Drizzle oil evenly over mixture, tossing to mix in oil well. Place flour and eggs in separate small bowls. Turn chicken pieces in flour, eggs and then in cereal mixture to coat well. Arrange chicken on a non-stick baking sheet. Bake at 375 degrees for 15 minutes, or until crisp and golden all over. For sauce, combine mustard and sauce. Serve chicken warm with sauce. Makes 4 to 6 servings.

...the Gobble-uns 'll git you
Ef you don't watch out!
-James Whitcomb Riley

Thankful Turkey Casserole

Beverly Stergeos
Mansfield, TX

My mom's favorite day-after-Thanksgiving casserole, made with whatever roast turkey was left over. My family always looks forward to this special dish...yum!

2 c. cooked turkey or chicken, cubed
1/2 c. onion, chopped
1/4 c. celery, chopped
2-oz. pkg. slivered almonds
8-oz. can water chestnuts, drained and chopped
10-3/4 oz. can cream of chicken soup
1 c. mayonnaise
Garnish: 1 c. round buttery crackers, crushed
cooked rice or egg noodles

Mix all ingredients except crackers and rice or noodles. Place in a lightly greased 2-quart casserole dish; top with crushed crackers. Bake, uncovered, at 350 degrees for about 20 minutes, until hot and bubbly. Serve over cooked rice or noodles. Serves 6 to 8.

Celebrate the spooky season...surround an orange pillar candle with candy corn in a glass hurricane.

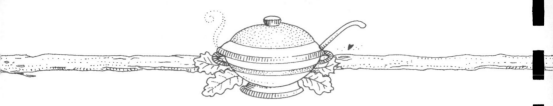

Fiesta Chicken Casserole

Janice O'Brien
Warrenton, VA

This quick-to-fix casserole is a real winner for busy school nights.

2 to 2-1/2 c. cooked chicken,
  diced
10-3/4 oz. can cream of chicken
  soup
1/2 c. sour cream

1/4 c. salsa
2 c. shredded Monterey Jack
  cheese, divided
2 c. corn chips, divided
Garnish: additional salsa

Combine chicken, soup, sour cream and salsa, mixing well. Spoon half the mixture into a lightly greased 1-1/2 quart casserole dish. Top with one cup cheese and one cup corn chips; repeat layers. Bake, uncovered, at 350 degrees for 20 to 25 minutes, or until heated through. Serve with additional salsa on the side. Serves 4.

An almost-instant centerpiece may be waiting in your backyard...just clip branches with colorful leaves or berries and tuck them into a tall vase.

Shoepeg Corn & Chiles

Kathleen Rampy
Midlothian, TX

My grandmother always made this casserole for the holidays.
I remember as a child first seeing the white shoepeg corn in this dish
and wondering about it...I thought corn only came in yellow!

8-oz. pkg. cream cheese,
   softened
1/2 c. milk
2 15-oz. cans shoepeg corn,
   drained
4-oz. can chopped green chiles

1/8 t. salt
1/8 t. pepper
1/8 t. cayenne pepper
1/8 t. garlic powder
Garnish: additional pepper,
   cayenne pepper

Melt cream cheese with milk in the top of a double boiler over hot water. Whisk until smooth and set aside. In a separate bowl, mix together corn, chiles and seasonings. Pour in cheese mixture; stir to mix well. Transfer to a buttered 2-quart casserole dish. Cover and bake at 325 degrees for 30 minutes. Uncover; sprinkle with additional seasoning as desired. Return to oven until lightly golden. Makes 6 servings.

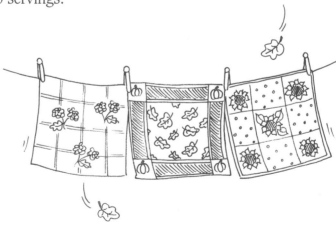

Whip up a batch of napkins in fun fall prints. Cut generous 20-inch squares of cotton fabric, hem the edges and stitch on rick rack in contrasting colors.

Rosemary Pork Chops

Diane Cohen
Kennesaw, GA

A scrumptious main dish with just five ingredients.

1/2 c. soy sauce
1/4 c. water
3 T. brown sugar, packed

1 T. dried rosemary
4 boneless pork chops

Combine soy sauce, water, brown sugar and rosemary in a large plastic zipping bag. Add pork chops and turn to coat; refrigerate for 3 hours. Drain and discard marinade. Arrange pork chops in a greased 11"x7" baking pan. Bake, uncovered, at 350 degrees for 30 to 35 minutes, until juices run clear. Makes 4 servings.

Freeze uncooked pork chops or chicken cutlets with marinade in freezer bags. After thawing overnight in the fridge, meat can go right into the baking pan or skillet for a scrumptious meal in a jiffy.

108

Queenie's Potato Deluxe

Paula Kane
Grand Blanc, MI

This potato dish is irresistible...one of my most popular recipes! Take it to any family get-together or potluck and you'll be bringing home an empty pan. Oh, and the name? My husband's nickname has always been Kingfish, so I'm called Queenie.

32-oz. pkg. plain or O'Brien
    frozen diced potatoes, thawed
1 c. onion, diced
10-3/4 oz. can cream of chicken
    soup
1 c. sour cream

1/2 c. butter, melted
8-oz. pkg. shredded sharp
    Cheddar cheese
salt and pepper to taste
Garnish: crushed potato chips

Mix all ingredients except potato chips in a large bowl. Transfer to a 13"x9" baking pan that has been sprayed with non-stick vegetable spray. Bake, covered, at 375 degrees for one hour. Uncover; top with crushed chips and return to oven for a few minutes, until golden. Makes 8 to 10 servings.

Make a tabletop Halloween tree! Choose a branch from the backyard. Spray it black, if you like, and stand it securely in a weighted vase. Wind with twinkling orange or purple lights...trim with spooky black crows, tiny ghosts made of white hankies and mini Jack-'O-Lanterns. Boo!

Party Ham Casserole

Barbara Reese
Catawissa, PA

This is very popular at parties and potlucks. My family loves mushrooms, so sometimes I add a large can of sliced and drained mushrooms in a layer before the second layer of noodles. Either way, it's a winner.

8-oz. pkg. medium egg noodles, uncooked and divided
10-3/4 oz. can cream of mushroom soup
1/2 c. milk
1 t. dried, minced onion
2 t. mustard
1 c. sour cream
2 c. cooked ham, cubed
1/4 c. dry bread crumbs
1-1/2 T. butter, melted
1 T. grated Parmesan cheese

Measure out half the noodles, reserving the rest for another recipe. Cook as package directs; drain. In a small saucepan, combine soup and milk, stirring over low heat until smooth. Add onion, mustard and sour cream, stirring to combine well. In a greased 1-1/2 quart casserole dish, layer half each of cooked noodles, ham and soup mixture; repeat layering. Toss bread crumbs with melted butter; sprinkle over casserole. Top with cheese. Bake, uncovered, at 350 degrees for 25 to 30 minutes, until golden. Makes 6 servings.

Autumn days seem to hurry by. Instead of a sit-down dinner with friends, why not plan a casual get-together? Potlucks are so easy...everyone brings along their favorite dish to share. It's all about food and fellowship!

Cowboy Dinner

Lisa Kastning
Lynnwood, WA

*Round up the family...this hearty dish will satisfy
the hungriest cowpoke!*

1 lb. ground beef
1/4 c. onion, chopped
1/2 c. celery, chopped
1/2 c. green pepper, chopped
15-oz. can pork & beans

1/2 c. barbecue sauce
salt and pepper to taste
11-oz. tube refrigerated bread
  sticks

Brown ground beef in a skillet; drain. Add onion, celery and green pepper; cook until vegetables are crisp-tender. Stir in beans, barbecue sauce, salt and pepper. Pour hot mixture into a greased 2-quart casserole dish. Gently unroll bread sticks; coil and lay across casserole to cover. Bake, uncovered, at 350 degrees for 20 to 25 minutes, until bubbly and bread sticks are golden. Serves 4 to 6.

Spread a cozy buffalo-check blanket on the dining table...
instant comfort on a damp and chilly day!

Brandi's Chicken & Artichokes

Brandi Talton
Guyton, GA

This is a favorite quick meal when I'm working late. Why settle for a fast food, when this is so easy to put together?

4 to 6 redskin potatoes, diced
14-oz. can artichokes, drained
  and chopped
3-lb. deli roast chicken,
  shredded
salt and pepper to taste

1 c. shredded Cheddar or
  mozzarella cheese
3 T. bacon bits
Optional: Parmesan peppercorn
  salad dressing to taste

Place potatoes in a microwave-safe container. Cover and microwave for 8 to 10 minutes, until almost tender. In a 9"x9" baking pan that has been sprayed with non-stick vegetable spray, layer potatoes, artichokes and chicken. Cover with aluminum foil; bake at 350 degrees for 15 minutes. Uncover and sprinkle with salt, pepper, cheese and bacon bits; drizzle with salad dressing, if desired. Bake for an additional 10 minutes, until heated through. Serves 4.

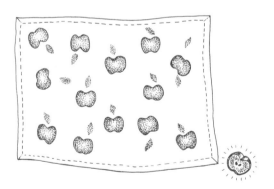

Make an apple print tablecloth...fun for the kids! Cut an apple in half, then pour fabric paint in a paper plate and let 'em stamp away on a plain tablecloth. Add leaves with an apple leaf shape cut from a kitchen sponge.

112

Creamy Zucchini Bake

Amy Woods
Collinsville, TX

If you like a crunchy topping, set aside 1/2 cup of the stuffing mix to crush and sprinkle over the dish.

6 c. zucchini, diced
1 c. carrots, peeled and
   shredded
1/2 to 1 c. onion, chopped
salt to taste
1 c. butter, melted

10-3/4 oz. can cream of chicken
   soup
6-oz. pkg. favorite-flavor
   stuffing mix
16-oz. container sour cream

In a large saucepan over medium heat, cover zucchini, carrots and onion with water. Add salt to taste. Boil for 5 minutes; drain. Blend melted butter, soup and stuffing mix; stir in sour cream. Carefully fold in drained vegetables. Pour into a lightly greased 2-quart casserole dish. Bake, uncovered, at 350 degrees for 30 minutes, until hot and bubbly. Makes 8 servings.

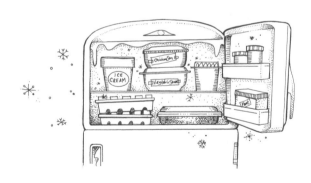

Get together with a girlfriend or two and spend a day making double batches of favorite casseroles to freeze. Your freezers will be full in no time!

113

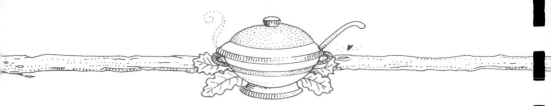

Baked Spaghetti

Jennifer Yandle
Indian Trail, NC

My kids love this! It's a great quick-to-fix dinner...
a hit at potlucks too.

1 lb. ground beef or ground pork sausage	26-oz. jar spaghetti sauce
1/2 c. onion, chopped	8-oz. pkg. spaghetti, cooked
1 c. green pepper, chopped	1 c. salami, chopped
1 clove garlic, minced	1 c. pepperoni, chopped
	1 c. shredded mozzarella cheese

Brown ground meat, onion, green pepper and garlic in a large skillet over medium heat; drain. Stir in spaghetti sauce; cover and simmer for 15 minutes. Mix in cooked spaghetti, salami and pepperoni. Transfer to a lightly greased 13"x9" baking pan; sprinkle with cheese. Bake, uncovered, at 350 degrees for 5 to 10 minutes, or until cheese is melted. Makes 6 to 8 servings.

Go barn sale-ing...you're sure to discover all kinds of
treasures and yummy homemade food too! Take along
some roomy tote bags for your purchases, plus a thermos
of hot cider and a snack or two to tide you over
until lunch. You'll have a ball!

Perfect Cheesy Pasta Bake

Marnie Calvert
Moore, OK

This is my husband's favorite dish. I have changed it several times, and he now proclaims the recipe is "perfect." It makes scrumptious leftovers too...enjoy!

16-oz. pkg. rotini pasta,
  uncooked
3-1/2 c. spaghetti sauce
1/2 c. grated Parmesan cheese
1 c. cooked chicken, diced

1/2 c. shredded mozzarella
  cheese
1/2 c. shredded pasteurized
  process cheese spread

Measure out 4 cups uncooked pasta, reserving the rest for another recipe. Cook pasta as package directs; drain and place in a large bowl. Add spaghetti sauce and Parmesan cheese; mix well. Transfer half of pasta mixture into a greased 8"x8" baking pan. Add chicken; cover with remaining pasta mixture. Top with cheeses. Bake, uncovered, at 350 degrees for 30 to 35 minutes, until hot and bubbly. Serves 4 to 6.

A welcome housewarming gift for a new neighbor! Prepare
a quick & easy family favorite in a new casserole dish...
enclose the recipe along with a note that says
the dish is theirs to keep.

Buttermilk Baked Chicken

Linda Foreman
Locust Grove, OK

This chicken is so juicy and tender! It's a favorite of my 91-year-old mother as well as my 8-year-old grandson. I like to use roasted garlic oil for extra flavor. Serve with mashed potatoes to really enjoy the delicious gravy...yum!

1/4 c. butter
1/4 c. oil
4 chicken breasts
1-1/2 c. buttermilk, divided
1 to 1-1/4 c. all-purpose flour
1/2 t. salt
1/2 t. pepper
1 t. paprika
1/2 t. garlic powder
1/2 t. Cajun seasoning
10-3/4 oz. can cream of
   mushroom soup

In a 13"x9" baking pan, melt butter with oil in a 425-degree oven. Dip chicken in 1/2 cup buttermilk; discard any buttermilk left over from dipping. Combine flour and seasonings; dredge chicken. Arrange chicken skin-side down in baking pan. Bake, uncovered, at 425 degrees for 30 minutes. Turn chicken over and continue to bake for 20 to 30 minutes, until chicken juices run clear. Stir together soup and remaining buttermilk; spoon over chicken. Cover; return to oven for an additional 10 minutes. Serve chicken drizzled with gravy from pan. Serves 4.

Savor a warm autumn evening by toting supper to the backyard. Kids can work up an appetite before dinner playing Tag or Hide-and-Seek. Afterwards, what could be better for dessert than marshmallows toasted over a fire ring?

Callie's Potato Casserole

Cindy McKinnon
El Dorado, AR

This was my Mamaw Callie's recipe. She would always fix these potatoes for Easter, but it's just as good any time of the year. She went to be with the Lord years ago and this is the only recipe of hers that I have written in her own handwriting. I photocopied the recipe onto pretty paper, framed it and hung it in my kitchen.

10-3/4 oz. can cream of
   mushroom soup
1 c. milk
4 to 6 redskin potatoes, peeled,
   cubed and boiled

1/2 c. green pepper, chopped
1/2 c. onion, chopped
salt and pepper to taste
1 c. shredded Cheddar cheese

Combine soup and milk in a bowl; stir well. Layer potatoes, pepper and onion in a 13"x9" baking pan sprayed with non-stick spray. Pour soup mixture on top. Sprinkle with salt and pepper to taste; add cheese on top. Cover with aluminum foil; bake at 300 degrees for 25 to 30 minutes. Serves 4 to 6.

Carry copies of favorite recipes with you so you can swing by the grocery and pick up the ingredients quickly and easily. Jot them on index cards and they'll fit right into a mini flip photo album.

Quick Turkey Cordon Bleu

Rebecca Barna
Blairsville, PA

This is a quick & tasty dinner recipe that I came up with...I've also made it in smaller portions for mini-appetizers.

1/2 lb. deli honey ham, sliced
   1/2-inch thick
1/2 lb. deli Swiss cheese, sliced
   1/2-inch thick
1/2 lb. deli smoked turkey
   breast, thinly sliced

2 12-oz. tubes refrigerated
   biscuits
2 eggs, beaten
1 to 1-1/2 c. Italian-flavored
   dry bread crumbs

Cut ham and cheese into 2-1/2-inch by 1/2-inch strips; cut turkey slices into thirds. Place a turkey piece on counter; top with a piece of ham and a piece of cheese. Roll turkey around ham and cheese. Flatten a biscuit and place turkey wrap on top. Roll biscuit around the turkey wrap as you would for stuffed cabbage, pinching seams to seal. Dip into beaten eggs, then bread crumbs. Place on an ungreased baking sheet. Repeat until all ingredients are used. Bake at 350 degrees for 35 to 40 minutes, or until golden. Serves 6.

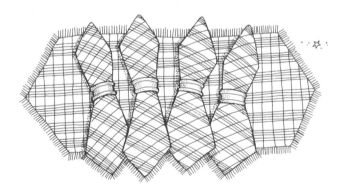

Whip up a new tablecloth or runner and matching napkins from homespun...no sewing needed! Choose fabric in warm seasonal colors like russet, brown and mustard. To add a fringe, just pull away threads, one row at a time.

118

Fiesta Skillet Chicken

Linda Quirk
Salinas, CA

*Turn this dish into Confetti Chicken in a jiffy...stir in small
drained cans of corn and black beans.*

8 boneless, skinless chicken
   thighs
1/4 c. oil
16-oz. jar mild or medium salsa
1-1/2 t. ground cumin

1/2 c. raisins
1/4 c. honey
1/8 t. cinnamon
cooked rice

In a large skillet over medium-high heat, brown chicken in oil; drain.
Mix remaining ingredients except rice in a medium bowl. Spoon over
chicken in skillet to coat each piece. Turn heat to medium-low and
cover; cook for 35 to 40 minutes. Serve over rice. Serves 4 to 6.

Fresh veggies don't need to be fussy. Set out a platter of
bite-size baby carrots, cherry tomatoes, broccoli flowerets
and celery stalks. Serve with a super-simple creamy dip
made by blending one cup cottage cheese, 1/4 cup plain
yogurt, one tablespoon minced onion, one teaspoon dried
parsley and 1/4 teaspoon dill weed. Yummy!

Speedy Shepherd's Pie

Angie Venable
Gooseberry Patch

*Hearty in a hurry! Use leftover mashed potatoes or pick up
a package of ready-to-serve potatoes.*

1 lb. ground beef, browned and
    drained
14-1/2 oz. can green beans,
    drained

8-oz. can tomato sauce
2 c. mashed potatoes
1 c. shredded Cheddar cheese

In a lightly greased 3-quart casserole dish, layer ingredients in order
given. Cover with aluminum foil. Bake at 350 degrees for 30 minutes,
until heated through and cheese is melted. Serves 6.

Show your spirit...dress up
a garden scarecrow in a
hometown football jersey!

Spuds & Sausages One-Dish

Sheri Mos
Independence, MO

I am notorious for throwing things together for dinner, usually to my family's dismay. This dish, though, was one everybody really liked! It's super easy, and now I get requests for it all the time. Very cozy and comforting.

4 c. boiling water
1 c. milk
1/4 c. butter, sliced
2 5-oz. pkgs. au gratin potatoes
   mix

16-oz. pkg. mini smoked
   sausages
Optional: shredded Cheddar
   cheese

Place boiling water, milk, butter and sauce mix in a greased 13"x9" baking pan; mix well. Stir in potatoes and sausages; top with cheese, if desired. Bake, uncovered, at 400 degrees for 35 minutes. Let stand for 5 minutes before serving. Makes 4 to 6 servings.

An old-fashioned bean pot becomes a perfect gift when
filled with packages of assorted dried beans and
a tried & true recipe for baked beans.

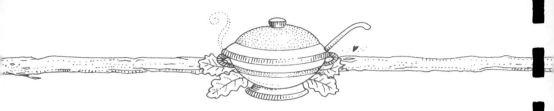

Hamburger Gravy & Potatoes

Peggy Donnally
Toledo, OH

My brother, Michael, has a big heart, an infectious laugh and the uncanny ability to turn childhood food memories into modern-day meals for his own family. This is his own tasty version of a quick dinner our mother used to make for us when we were young.

1-1/2 lbs. ground beef round	salt and pepper to taste
1 onion, finely chopped	1/2 lb. sliced mushrooms
1 t. onion powder	2 12-oz. jars beef gravy
1/2 t. garlic powder	mashed potatoes

Brown beef in a large skillet over medium heat; drain. Add onion and seasonings to skillet. Cook over medium-low heat until onion is translucent. Stir in mushrooms and gravy; cover and simmer for 10 minutes. Ladle over mashed potatoes. Serves 6.

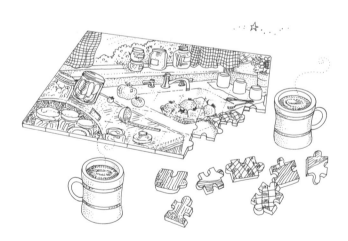

Family night! Serve a simple supper, then spend the evening playing favorite board games or assembling jigsaw puzzles together.

122

World-Famous Green Beans

Ingrid Shewmake
Joplin, MO

My mother-in-law has always treated me like her own daughter and been a great teacher to me in the art of cooking. This simple recipe has started my husband bragging on my cooking many a time...when actually I got the secret from his mom!

4 15-oz. cans green beans
6 to 8 cubes beef bouillon
1/2 c. butter, sliced

1/2 c. onion, finely chopped
pepper to taste
Optional: 1/2 c. bacon bits

Combine all ingredients in a medium saucepan over medium heat. Bring to a rolling boil; reduce heat to medium-low and simmer for 20 to 30 minutes. Serves 6.

Create a fall centerpiece in a snap! Hot-glue ears of mini Indian corn around a terra cotta pot and set a vase of orange or yellow mums in the center.

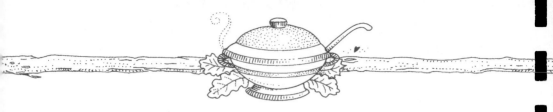

Patti's Macaroni Casserole

Patti Lewandowski
Sylvania, OH

*My mom named this casserole after me because it was my favorite...
it's the ultimate comfort food! She would make it every year for
my birthday. Now my own family likes it too.*

7-1/4 oz. pkg. macaroni &
   cheese mix
1 lb. ground beef chuck
1/2 T. dried, minced onion

2 T. margarine
10-3/4 oz. cream of mushroom
   soup
1/2 c. milk

Prepare macaroni & cheese as directed on package; set aside.
Meanwhile, in a skillet over medium heat, brown ground beef and
onion in margarine. Stir in soup and milk. Add beef mixture to
prepared macaroni & cheese and mix well. Transfer to a greased
1-1/2 quart casserole dish. Bake, uncovered, at 350 degrees for
25 minutes. Serves 4 to 6.

Spoon mac & cheese or other favorite casseroles into
individual ramekins for baking...perfect for busy
fall evenings when everyone is coming & going
at different times!

Mrs. Morris' Hot Chicken Salad
Nancy Hutchins
Eagles Mere, PA

Mrs. Morris was a neighbor of ours when I was growing up. She was a lifelong friend of my mom, a very jovial lady with a great smile. Mrs. Morris was always cooking and had some really tasty recipes which she shared willingly...this is one of the best!

6-oz. pkg. long-grain and wild rice, cooked
4 c. cooked chicken breast, diced
1-1/2 c. celery, chopped
1 onion, minced
1 c. mayonnaise
2 10-3/4 oz. cans cream of chicken soup

1 t. salt
4 eggs, hard-boiled, peeled and chopped
Optional: 1 c. potato chips, crushed, or seasoned dry bread crumbs
Optional: 1 c. shredded Cheddar cheese

In a large bowl, combine all ingredients except optional ones; mix well. Place in a buttered 3-quart casserole dish. If desired, cover top of casserole with crushed potato chips or bread crumbs and/or cheese. Bake, uncovered, at 400 degrees for 30 minutes. Serves 4 to 6.

In early autumn, before the busy holiday season begins, why not invite friends to a crafting get-together? Choose a simple craft like ornaments or package tie-ons. You provide craft materials, a work table and a beverage...guests bring a goodie to share. Everyone is sure to have a wonderful time!

My Three Veggies Dish

Judy Lange
Imperial, PA

*I enjoy making this for baby showers, wedding showers or just
a plain old get-together...it's always a hit!*

16-oz. pkg. frozen broccoli
16-oz. pkg. Brussels sprouts
16-oz. pkg. frozen cauliflower
10-3/4 oz. can cream of
  mushroom soup

8-oz. jar pasteurized process
  cheese sauce
2.8-oz. can French fried onions

Combine frozen vegetables in a large saucepan; cover with water.
Bring to a boil over medium-high heat. Boil for about 5 minutes; drain
well. Transfer vegetables to a buttered 10"x8" baking pan. Combine
soup and cheese sauce; spread over vegetables. Sprinkle onions over
top. Bake, uncovered, at 350 degrees for about 30 minutes. Makes
10 servings.

Just for fun, serve up soft pretzels instead of dinner rolls.
Twist strips of refrigerated bread stick dough into pretzel
shapes and place on an ungreased baking sheet. Brush
with beaten egg white, sprinkle with coarse salt
and bake as directed.

Aunt Ruby's Sweet Potatoes

Jonie Karns
Urbandale, IA

I got this recipe over 20 years ago from our neighbors back in Alabama.
It has been a tradition at our house every Thanksgiving and
Christmas dinner ever since.

3 c. sweet potatoes, peeled,
   cooked and mashed
1 c. sugar
1/2 c. butter, melted

2 eggs, beaten
1 t. vanilla extract
1/3 c. milk

Mix all ingredients together. Spoon into a greased 13"x9" baking pan.
Sprinkle with Brown Sugar Topping. Bake, uncovered, at 350 degrees
for 25 to 30 minutes. Serves 8.

Brown Sugar Topping:

1 c. brown sugar, packed
1/2 c. all-purpose flour

1/3 c. butter, softened
1 c. chopped nuts

Combine ingredients; mix well.

Set up a hay maze in the backyard. Stack bales of hay or
straw and make a little path that runs through them...
grownups will have as much fun as kids, trying to
follow all the twists and turns!

Smothered Mushrooms

Jen Eveland-Kupp
Blandon, PA

Luscious spooned over a juicy steak...yummy on baked potatoes too.

16-oz. pkg. mushrooms
3-1/2 T. all-purpose flour
1-1/2 t. chicken bouillon
   granules
1 c. milk

1/8 t. hot pepper sauce
2 T. fresh chives, chopped
   and divided
Garnish: 1/3 c. sour cream

Arrange mushrooms in an ungreased 1-1/2 quart casserole dish; set aside. Combine flour and bouillon in a small saucepan. Gradually add milk, stirring over medium-low heat until smooth. Add hot pepper sauce and one tablespoon chives. Cook over medium heat, stirring constantly, until thickened and bubbly. Pour mixture over mushrooms. Bake, uncovered, at 350 degrees for 25 minutes. Remove from oven; dollop with sour cream and sprinkle with remaining chives. Makes 6 servings.

Set a photo placecard at each person's place setting. Decorate small picture frames with short cinnamon sticks glued on to form a square. Add a tiny pine cone to one corner for an accent.

Creamed Chicken on Toast

Carrie Porder
Woonsocket, RI

This recipe dates from many years ago, when my mother-in-law was a young girl and her mother needed an easy dinner to serve. My grandmother-in-law never really liked to cook much, so what she served was plain & simple. She turned 102 years old this past January, so her cooking could not have been too bad! My mother-in-law and I have both adapted it for our own families. Serve it over rice or noodles, if you like.

4 to 6 boneless, skinless
   chicken breasts, cut into
   bite-size pieces
1 onion, chopped
pepper and dried sage to taste
2 10-3/4 oz. cans cream of
   chicken soup
2 10-3/4 oz. cans cream of
   mushroom soup

2 10-3/4 oz. cans cream of
   celery soup
2 4-oz. cans mushroom stems
   and pieces
2 4-oz. cans young peas
Optional: salt to taste
4 to 8 slices bread, toasted

Place chicken in a lightly greased large stockpot; add onion, pepper and sage. Cover and cook over medium-high heat, stirring often, until chicken is no longer pink and juices run clear. If a thicker consistency is desired, drain juices from stockpot. Add soups, mushrooms and peas; stir well. Reduce heat to medium. Cook, stirring often, until heated through and flavors have blended, about 15 minutes. If desired, add salt to taste. Serve spooned over warm toast. Serves 4 to 6.

Fleece fabric can be found in lots of whimsical patterns and bright colors...why not stitch up an armload of warm fringed scarves for your family?

Creamy Broccoli Casserole

Sharon Brown
Orange Park, FL

Even the fussiest eaters will ask for seconds!

2 10-oz. pkgs. frozen broccoli,
  cooked and drained
2 T. butter
2 T. all-purpose flour
1 t. chicken bouillon granules
3/4 c. milk

1/2 c. cream cheese, softened
1/4 t. salt
Optional: green onion, chopped,
  to taste
1/2 c. shredded Cheddar cheese

Arrange broccoli in a lightly greased shallow 9"x9" baking pan; set aside. Melt butter in a small saucepan over low heat; add flour, stirring until smooth. Add bouillon and milk; stir until thickened. Blend in cream cheese, salt and onion, if using, until smooth. Spoon sauce over broccoli; sprinkle shredded cheese over top. Cover with aluminum foil; bake at 350 degrees for 30 minutes. Uncover; continue to bake for 5 to 10 minutes. Serves 4.

For the easiest-ever fall centerpiece, slip a pot of asters
into a vintage wooden pail.

130

Good-On-Anything Veggie Sauce
Sharon Velenosi
Stanton, CA

I've served this tasty, healthy sauce over baked or broiled chicken, pasta and even rice. It can be stirred up in a jiffy and even freezes well.

1/4 c. olive oil
3 cloves garlic, minced
1 onion, chopped
2 zucchini, chopped

1/4 c. fresh parsley, chopped
1/4 c. fresh basil, chopped
2 28-oz. cans crushed tomatoes
salt and pepper to taste

In a large saucepan, heat oil over medium heat. Add garlic, onion and zucchini. Cook, stirring, for about 5 minutes. Add remaining ingredients. Simmer for 25 minutes, stirring frequently. Makes about 6 cups.

A turban squash makes an amusing flower vase...try other hard winter squashes too! Cut an opening at the top of the squash and slip in a small plastic cup or a floral tube. Fill with flowers and add water to keep them fresh.

Reuben Casserole

Suzanne Ruminski
Johnson City, NY

An easy version of everyone's favorite hot deli sandwich that's always a hit...yummy and filling!

16-oz. can sauerkraut
12-oz. can corned beef, crumbled
2 c. shredded Swiss cheese
1/2 c. mayonnaise
1/4 c. Thousand Island salad dressing

2 c. tomatoes, sliced
1/4 to 1/2 c. pumpernickel or rye bread crumbs
2 T. butter, melted

Place undrained sauerkraut in a greased 1-1/2 quart casserole dish. Top with corned beef and cheese. Combine mayonnaise and salad dressing; spread over cheese. Arrange tomatoes on top. Toss together bread crumbs and melted butter; sprinkle over top of casserole. Bake, uncovered, at 350 degrees for 45 minutes. Let stand briefly before serving. Makes 6 servings.

Fallen leaf art is fun for the whole family. Choose colorful leaves and press them in a book between pieces of wax paper for a few days. Glue leaves to construction or scrapbook paper to form a picture...twigs, seed pods and acorn caps can be added too. Finish by drawing or painting on details.

A
Bountiful

Family Feast

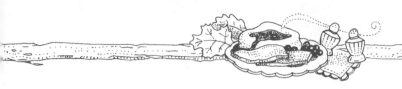

Dijon Roast Turkey

Claire Bertram
Lexington, KY

It just wouldn't be Thanksgiving without a scrumptious golden roast turkey! This one is extra-special, served with a savory herbed cream sauce. We like to drizzle the sauce over roasted asparagus and Brussels sprouts too.

12 to 14-lb. turkey, thawed if
    frozen

1/3 c. Dijon mustard, divided
2 T. olive oil

Pat turkey dry with paper towels. Remove neck and giblets from turkey; reserve for another use. Place turkey breast-side up on a rack in a large roaster pan. Spread 2 tablespoons mustard inside turkey. Loosen skin over breast; spread remaining mustard under skin. Smooth loosened skin back into place; hold in place with toothpicks. Tuck in legs and wings. Insert a meat thermometer into thickest part of thigh. Brush oil over turkey. Roast at 325 degrees for 3-1/2 to 3-3/4 hours, until thermometer reads 165 degrees. When skin is golden, tent loosely with aluminum foil to prevent overbrowning. Let stand for 20 minutes before slicing. Serve with Dijon Cream Sauce. Makes 10 to 12 servings.

Dijon Cream Sauce:

reserved turkey pan drippings
3 T. all-purpose flour
1 c. half-and-half

1/4 c. Dijon mustard
1/4 c. fresh parsley, chopped

Pour drippings into a 2-cup measuring cup; chill for 10 minutes. Skim and discard fat. Add water to drippings to equal 2 cups; pour into a saucepan over medium-high heat. Whisk in flour; cook and stir until mixture thickens and begins to boil. Stir in remaining ingredients. Reduce heat to medium; cook and stir without boiling until thickened. Makes about 3-1/2 cups.

A Bountiful Family Feast

Grandma's Buttery Mashed Potatoes
J.J. Presley
Portland, TX

Grandma used to make these mashed potatoes every Sunday for lunch, no matter what the main course was. I can still taste them to this day!

6 to 8 potatoes, peeled and
    cubed
1/2 c. butter, softened

1 c. evaporated milk
salt and pepper to taste

Cover potatoes with water in a large saucepan; bring to a boil over medium-high heat. Cook until tender, about 15 minutes; drain. Add remaining ingredients. Beat with an electric mixer on medium speed until blended and creamy. Serves 8 to 12.

Rich Turkey Gravy
Tina Wright
Atlanta, GA

This easy recipe takes the mystery out of gravy making.

1/4 c. turkey pan drippings
1/4 c. all-purpose flour

2 c. milk or water
2 t. chicken bouillon granules

Pour drippings into a skillet over medium heat. Stir flour into drippings; cook and stir until dark golden. Stir in milk or water and bouillon. Reduce heat slightly; cook and stir until thickened and bouillon has dissolved. Makes about 1-1/2 cups.

Sweet, little servings of butter for a festive table are oh-so easy to make. Press softened butter into decorative candy molds, then chill and pop out.

135

Hearty Autumn Stew

Nichole Martelli
Alvin, TX

With the temperatures getting colder, I wanted to fill the slow cooker with a flavorful, satisfying stew to warm the tummies of my family after a long day of school and work. Everyone at the dinner table just loved it.

1/2 butternut squash, peeled
   and cubed
3 carrots, peeled and diced
3 stalks celery, diced
1/2 onion, diced
10-oz. can diced tomatoes with
   chiles
1-1/2 lbs. stew beef, cubed
1/4 to 1/2 c. all-purpose flour

10-3/4 oz. can cream of
   mushroom soup
1.35-oz. pkg. onion soup mix
1 T. seafood seasoning
1 T. Italian seasoning
1/4 t. garlic powder
salt and pepper to taste
cooked rice

Place vegetables in a 5 to 6-quart slow cooker. Dredge beef in flour and add to slow cooker. Top with remaining ingredients except rice. Add enough water to fill slow cooker 2/3 full. Cover and cook on low setting for 8 to 10 hours. Stir before serving; spoon over cooked rice. Serves 8 to 10.

Repurpose gourds and mini pumpkins left over from Halloween...spray them gold with craft paint to tuck into harvest centerpieces.

A Bountiful Family Feast

Anne's Chicken & Dried Beef

Marilyn Wintle
Fort Myers, FL

A co-worker shared this easy-yet-elegant recipe with me.

2-1/4 oz. jar dried beef
4 boneless, skinless chicken
   breasts
salt, pepper, garlic powder and
   onion powder to taste
10-3/4 oz. can cream of
   chicken soup

8-oz. container sour cream
8 slices bacon
salt and pepper to taste
cooked rice

Arrange dried beef to cover the bottom of a greased 13"x9" baking pan. Sprinkle chicken with seasonings; place on top of beef. Mix together soup and sour cream; pour over chicken. Top with bacon slices. Bake, covered, at 350 degrees for 30 minutes, or until chicken is cooked through. If bacon is not crisp yet, place under broiler for 2 to 3 minutes. Serve over cooked rice. Serves 4.

On Turkey Day, there's really no need for fancy appetizers... just set out a bowl of unshelled walnuts or pecans and a nutcracker! Guests will busy themselves cracking nuts to snack on while you put the finishing touches on dinner.

Pumpkin-Sausage Penne

Michelle Christensen
West Jordan, UT

I started making this delicious casserole years ago as a Halloween night meal. It's since become a family favorite that gets requested all through autumn and winter.

8-oz. pkg. cream cheese, cubed
2/3 c. grated Parmesan cheese
1/2 c. butter, sliced
1/2 c. milk
1 c. canned pumpkin
1/2 t. cayenne pepper
nutmeg to taste

16-oz. penne pasta, cooked
16-oz. pkg. maple-flavored
   ground pork sausage,
   browned and drained
Optional: additional grated
   Parmesan cheese

Combine cream cheese, Parmesan cheese, butter and milk in a large saucepan. Cook over low heat until cream cheese is melted, stirring frequently. Stir in pumpkin and spices; cook until heated through, stirring occasionally. Add cooked pasta and sausage; toss lightly. Serve topped with additional Parmesan cheese, if desired. Makes 8 servings.

Are you hosting a large Thanksgiving gathering? A day or two before the big day, set out all the serving platters, baskets and dishes and label them..."Roast Turkey," "Aunt Jane's Pumpkin Muffins" and so on. When the time arrives, you'll be able to put dinner on the table in a jiffy.

A Bountiful Family Feast

Janice's Cranberry Sauce

Janice Shear
Locust Valley, NY

When I was a teenager, my sister Laura Jean, then 3, was overwhelmed by the sight of the roast turkey when it came out of the oven. She said it was so beautiful, she wanted to kiss it. After it had cooled a bit, I lifted her up and she did give it a kiss! Since then, it has been our tradition that the youngest child in the family kisses the Thanksgiving turkey before it is carved. This year Laura Jean's son Aaron did the honors.

12-oz. pkg. cranberries
1 c. sugar
2/3 c. water
1/3 c. orange juice

zest of 1 orange
1 c. walnuts, broken
2 t. cinnamon

Combine first 5 ingredients in a saucepan. Bring to a boil over low heat, stirring constantly. Cook until mixture begins to thicken, about 5 minutes. Add nuts and cinnamon; cook for another 2 minutes. Chill at least one hour before serving. Makes 2-1/2 cups.

Roasted Asparagus & Squash

Marion Sundberg
Ramona, CA

Either fresh or frozen veggies can be used in this unusual side dish.

1 butternut squash, peeled and
   chopped
1 lb. asparagus, cut into 1-inch
   pieces

2 T. olive oil
1 clove garlic, minced
salt and pepper to taste

Toss all ingredients together; spread in a lightly greased 15"x10" jelly-roll pan. Bake, uncovered, at 350 degrees for 45 to 60 minutes, or until golden and tender. Serves 6 to 8.

So simple...dress up the stems of water glasses
with a few twigs of bittersweet berries.

139

Pork Chops in Mushroom Sauce

Sue Hecht
Roselle Park, NJ

Serve these pork chops with buttery mashed potatoes
to really enjoy the flavorful sauce.

8 pork chops
1/2 c. all-purpose flour
pepper to taste
2 T. butter
1/2 c. green onions, chopped

2 cloves garlic, minced
1 c. sliced mushrooms
1/2 t. dried thyme
1 c. pale ale or chicken broth

Dredge pork chops in flour and pepper. In a large skillet over medium-high heat, melt butter until it foams. Add pork chops; brown well on both sides. Remove pork chops from skillet and set aside. Add onions and garlic to skillet; sauté for 2 minutes. Add mushrooms and thyme; sauté an additional 3 minutes. Return pork chops to skillet; add ale or broth and bring to a boil. Reduce heat to low; cover and simmer for one hour. Transfer pork chops to a warm serving plate; skim fat from sauce in skillet. Serve with sauce spooned over pork chops. Serves 4 to 6.

For whimsical napkin rings, tie ears of red-kerneled
strawberry popcorn with a raffia bow and
lay on folded napkins.

Vermont Maple Chicken

Paula Spadaccini
Shelburne, VT

*A delicious old New England farmhouse recipe that I have modernized
for ease of preparation. Be sure to use pure maple syrup
for the best flavor.*

1/4 c. all-purpose flour
salt and pepper to taste
4 boneless, skinless chicken
    breasts
2 T. butter
1/2 c. maple syrup

1 t. dried sage
1/2 t. dried thyme
1/4 t. dried marjoram
1 Spanish onion, sliced
1/2 c. water

Place flour, salt and pepper in a plastic zipping bag. Add chicken to
bag and shake to coat evenly; set aside. Melt butter over medium-
high heat in an oven-safe skillet. Cook chicken until lightly browned.
Remove skillet from heat. Drizzle syrup over chicken, turning to coat
completely. Sprinkle chicken with herbs; place onion slices on top to
cover chicken. Add water to skillet. Bake, uncovered, at 350 degrees
for 30 minutes. Turn chicken over; continue baking for an additional
15 to 20 minutes. Serves 4.

Candied cranberries are a lovely garnish for roast turkey or
chicken. In a saucepan, bring one cup water and one cup
sugar almost to a boil, stirring until sugar dissolves. Pour
into a bowl and add one cup fresh cranberries; chill
overnight. Drain cranberries well. Toss with superfine
sugar to coat and dry on wax paper.

Grandma's Spaghetti Casserole

Karen MacCauley
Trumbauersville, PA

As kids, we loved this warm comfort-food casserole and requested it whenever we visited our grandparents.

2 8-oz. pkgs. spaghetti, uncooked
1/2 c. butter
2 onions, chopped
1 green pepper, chopped
1-1/2 lbs. ground beef
2 10-3/4 oz. cans tomato soup

1/2 c. water
2 t. Worcestershire sauce
8-oz. pkg. shredded mozzarella cheese
Optional: grated Parmesan cheese

Measure out 1-1/2 packages of spaghetti, reserving the rest for another recipe. Cook as package directs; drain. Meanwhile, melt butter in a large skillet over medium heat; sauté onions and green pepper. Add ground beef and brown; drain. Add soup, water and Worcestershire sauce to skillet; mix well. Add cooked spaghetti; stir until evenly coated with sauce. Transfer to a well-greased 3-quart casserole dish; top with mozzarella cheese. Bake, uncovered, for one hour at 350 degrees. Sprinkle servings with Parmesan cheese, if desired. Serves 4 to 6.

Share the Thanksgiving bounty...call a local college and invite an out-of-town student to dinner who won't be going home over the long weekend.

A Bountiful Family Feast

Savory Shrimp & Pasta Toss

Kathleen Neff
Claxton, GA

Add a crisp tossed salad and a basket of warm garlic bread for
an easy, elegant meal with friends.

12-oz. pkg. penne pasta,
   divided
2 t. olive oil
1 onion, chopped
28-oz. can diced tomatoes
1/4 t. red pepper flakes

1/4 t. dried oregano
1 lb. uncooked medium shrimp,
   peeled and cleaned
1/4 c. fresh parsley, chopped
4-oz. pkg. crumbled feta cheese,
   divided

Measure out half the package of pasta, reserving the rest for another
recipe. Cook as package directs; drain. Meanwhile, in a large heavy
skillet, heat oil over medium heat. Add onion; cook until tender and
lightly golden. Stir in tomatoes and their juice, red pepper flakes and
oregano; cook until boiling over high heat. Reduce heat to medium;
cook sauce until slightly thickened, stirring occasionally. Stir in
shrimp; cook for 2 to 4 minutes, until pink. Remove skillet from heat;
stir in parsley and 1/2 cup feta cheese. Add cooked pasta to skillet
mixture and toss to coat. Use remaining cheese to top each serving.
Serves 4.

Grouped on a table or buffet, a mix of old and new lanterns
greets guests with the warm glow of candlelight.

143

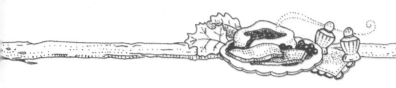

Rolled Flank Steak

Cathy Hillier
Salt Lake City, UT

A cozy dinner for an evening when it's just the two of you.

1/2 lb. beef flank steak
2 T. butter, divided
1/4 c. onion
1/4 c. celery, sliced
1/4 c. plain croutons
1/4 c. grated Parmesan cheese

2 T. water
1/4 t. dried basil
8-oz. can tomato sauce
Optional: additional grated
    Parmesan cheese

Slice steak horizontally in half, being careful not to cut all the way through. Open steak; set aside. Melt one tablespoon butter in a skillet over medium-high heat. Add onion and celery; cook and stir until crisp-tender. Add croutons, cheese, water and basil; toss to mix. Remove from heat; spread mixture over bottom half of steak. Roll up steak jelly-roll style; tie with kitchen string. Melt remaining butter in same skillet; brown steak evenly on all sides. Pour tomato sauce over steak. Reduce heat to low; cover and simmer for one hour and 30 minutes to 2 hours, or until steak is tender, occasionally spooning sauce over steak. Slice steak; serve topped with sauce and additional cheese, if desired. Serves 2.

Try a fun new activity after the last dish is passed...a family scavenger hunt! Make up lists of items that might be spotted on a walk around the neighborhood...a spotted dog, a round rock, a leftover Halloween pumpkin. Then divide up into teams and go! Everyone will have a blast and they'll walk off that "too much of a good thing" feeling.

144

Lori's Best Brussels Sprouts

Barbara Dell
Bethpage, NY

I never would eat Brussels sprouts until my sister tricked my 7-year-old niece Emily and me with this recipe..to my surprise, these sprouts were delicious! Now I even fix them myself.

1 lb. Brussels sprouts, trimmed
1-1/2 tsp. olive oil
1 t. garlic, minced

1 T. Italian-seasoned dry bread crumbs

Cover Brussels sprouts with water in a medium saucepan. Bring to a boil over medium heat; simmer until tender, about 7 to 8 minutes. Drain. Heat oil and garlic in a sauté pan until sizzling; add sprouts and sauté for one minute. Add bread crumbs, stirring until combined and heated through. Makes 4 servings.

Wild Rice & Mushrooms

Samantha Starks
Madison, WI

This slow-cooker recipe is scrumptious and it feeds a crowd!

10-1/2 oz. can beef consommé
10-1/2 oz. can French onion soup
2-1/4 c. water
1/2 c. butter, melted

13-1/4 oz. can sliced mushrooms, drained
1 c. wild rice, uncooked
1 c. long-cooking brown rice, uncooked

Combine all ingredients in a slow cooker; stir well. Cover and cook on low setting for 7 to 8 hours, until rice is tender. Serves 10 to 12.

Stock up on Chinese take-out containers...they're just right for sending home Turkey Day leftovers with guests.

145

Dad's Best Mac & Cheese

Kathy Slevoski
Georgetown, MA

This recipe was given to me by my father, Mark Savage, who passed away several years ago. It was always a family favorite to make, trying different cheeses...some sharp, or not so sharp, or REALLY sharp! Buttering the dish makes the outer edges of the casserole nice and crusty...yum!

8-oz. pkg. elbow macaroni,
   uncooked
1 egg, beaten
1 T. hot water
1 t. dry mustard

1 t. salt
1 c. milk
12-oz. pkg. shredded sharp
   Cheddar cheese, divided
1 T. butter, softened

Cook macaroni according to package directions; drain and return to pan. Beat egg, water, mustard and salt together; add to macaroni. Pour in milk and stir well. Add most of cheese, reserving enough to sprinkle on top. Spread butter in a 2-quart casserole dish; pour macaroni mixture into dish. Sprinkle with reserved cheese. Bake, uncovered, at 350 degrees for 35 to 45 minutes, until top is golden. Makes 6 to 8 servings.

Forced flowers offer a little bit of springtime as the weather cools. Fill vintage bulb vases with water, set in a warm sunny window and drop a narcissus bulb into each one. You'll see blooming flowers in just a few weeks.

Southern Hashbrown Casserole

Sarah Crowder
McKinney, TX

If you have never tried these potatoes, don't wait a minute longer.
This is my most-requested recipe at all of our Bible study potlucks...
I can never make enough!

16-oz. container sour cream
10-3/4 oz. can cream of chicken
  soup
3/4 c. butter, melted and divided
1 t. salt
1 T. onion, minced

8-oz. pkg. shredded Cheddar
  cheese
32-oz. pkg. frozen southern
  diced potatoes, thawed and
  drained
2 c. corn flake cereal, crushed

Combine sour cream, soup and 1/2 cup butter in a large bowl; mix well. Add salt, onion and cheese; blend in potatoes and stir well. Pour mixture into a lightly greased shallow 2-quart casserole dish. Toss together cereal and remaining butter; sprinkle over potatoes. Bake, uncovered, at 350 degrees for about 50 minutes, until golden and bubbly. Serves 8.

Ask family & friends to share a copy of tried & true recipe
favorites and create a holiday cookbook...a great gift
for a new cook in the family.

Caramelized Onion Pot Roast

Nancy Girard
Chesapeake, VA

One of my favorite slow-cooker recipes! Long, slow cooking transforms a budget-friendly roast into a scrumptious meal that's good enough to serve to company.

2 T. oil, divided
2-1/2 lb. boneless beef chuck
   roast
salt and pepper to taste
4 onions, sliced

1 c. beef broth
1/2 c. apple juice
1 T. brown sugar, packed
1 T. cider vinegar
2 T. Dijon mustard

Heat one tablespoon oil in a large frying pan over medium-high heat. Brown roast on all sides. Remove to a plate; sprinkle with salt and pepper to taste. Add remaining oil to pan and cook onions until deep golden, stirring frequently. Add broth, juice, brown sugar, vinegar and mustard to onions in pan. Spoon half of onion mixture into a slow cooker; place roast on top. Top with remaining onion mixture. Cover and cook on low setting for 8 to 9 hours. Serves 6.

Keep little ones busy and happy with a crafting area while the grown-ups put the finishing touches on Thanksgiving dinner. Set out paper plates to decorate with colored paper, feathers, pom-poms, crayons and washable glue. At dinnertime, they'll be proud to display their creations!

148

Hearty Sauerkraut Platter

Jill Duvendack
Pioneer, OH

Wonderful for cool-weather entertaining...will satisfy even the heartiest appetites. Serve with spicy brown mustard and homestyle chunky applesauce on the side.

1 lb. thick-sliced bacon
3 onions, finely diced
3 cloves garlic
5 lbs. sauerkraut, drained and divided
4 smoked ham hocks, divided
salt and pepper to taste

2 bay leaves
2 qts. water
2 Polish garlic sausage links, sliced into 2-inch pieces
8 smoked pork chops
8 knackwursts or frankfurters
8 to 10 redskin potatoes

In a large skillet over medium-high heat, fry bacon until crisp. Remove bacon to a plate. Add onions and garlic to drippings in skillet; cook until golden. Remove and set aside. Place 1/3 of sauerkraut in an ungreased deep roaster; layer with 2 ham hocks, half of bacon, half of onion mixture, salt and pepper to taste. Repeat layers, ending with remaining sauerkraut. Enclose bay leaves in a cheesecloth bag and place on top. Pour water into roaster; cover and bake at 400 degrees for 3 hours. Arrange garlic sausage and pork chops on top of sauerkraut; cover and continue baking for 30 minutes. Shortly before serving time, steam knackwursts or frankfurters and potatoes until tender. To serve, spoon sauerkraut onto a large platter. Discard bay leaves. Arrange meats over sauerkraut, with potatoes placed around edge of platter. Makes 8 to 10 servings.

Fill a toy wheelbarrow with gourds or mini Indian corn ears...so sweet on a sideboard.

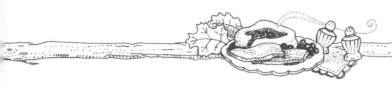

Honey-Glazed Chicken

*Joan White
Malvern, PA*

*It just takes a pinch of this & a dash of that to cook up the juiciest,
best-tasting roast chicken ever!*

1/2 c. all-purpose flour
1 t. salt
1/4 t. cayenne pepper
3 lbs. chicken
1/2 c. butter, melted and divided

1/4 c. honey
1/4 c. brown sugar, packed
1/4 c. lemon juice
1 T. soy sauce
1-1/2 t. curry powder

In a large bowl or plastic zipping bag, combine flour, salt and cayenne pepper. Add chicken pieces and shake to coat. Pour 1/4 cup melted butter into a 13"x9" baking pan. Arrange chicken in pan, turning once to coat. Bake, uncovered, at 350 degrees for 30 minutes. Combine honey, brown sugar, lemon juice, soy sauce, curry powder and remaining butter; mix well and pour over chicken. Bake an additional 35 to 40 minutes, basting several times with pan drippings, until chicken is golden and thoroughly cooked. Serves 4 to 6.

Put a slow cooker to work turning the leftovers of the holiday bird into flavorful broth for soup. Place the bones in a large slow cooker, breaking to fit if necessary. Add onion, celery, carrots and enough water to fill 2/3 full. Cover and cook on low for about 10 hours. Strain broth with a colander and refrigerate or freeze.

150

Sweet Potato-Apple Bake

Beatrix Dugat
Portland, TX

The second year we were married, my husband and I were unable to go home for Thanksgiving so I cooked dinner for the two of us. A friend had shared this yummy side dish recipe and we loved it...I have been making it for holidays for 32 years now!

3 c. sweet potatoes, peeled, cooked and mashed
1/2 c. sugar
2 eggs, beaten
7 T. margarine, melted and divided
1/2 c. milk

1-1/2 t. vanilla extract
1/2 t. salt
3 apples, cored, peeled and sliced
3/4 c. brown sugar, packed
1/2 c. chopped pecans
1 t. cinnamon

Combine sweet potatoes, sugar, eggs, 4 tablespoons melted margarine, milk, vanilla and salt; set aside. In a separate bowl, combine apples, brown sugar, pecans, cinnamon and enough of remaining margarine to moisten. Layer half the sweet potato mixture in a greased 13"x9" baking pan. Spoon apple mixture over top; spread remaining sweet potato mixture over apple mixture. Spread Pecan Topping over top. Bake, uncovered, at 350 degrees for 30 to 45 minutes. Serves 8.

Pecan Topping:

1/2 c. brown sugar, packed
1/3 c. all-purpose flour

1 c. chopped pecans
2 to 3 T. margarine, melted

Combine all ingredients; toss to mix.

Come, ye thankful people, come,
Raise the song of harvest home!
-Henry Alford

151

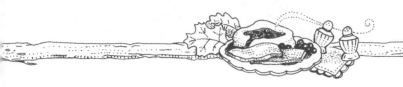

Carolina Garden Stew

Tabetha Stone
Eastover, NC

*A woman whom I knew for 20 years gave me this delicious recipe.
She taught me so many wonderful recipes. She was our local colorful
character and a wonderfully sweet woman.*

2 qts. beef broth or water
2 to 3 lbs. stew beef, cubed
3 to 4 potatoes, peeled and
    cubed
2 onions, cubed
4 carrots, sliced 1/2-inch thick
2 to 3 stalks celery, sliced
    1/2-inch thick

1 green, yellow or red pepper,
    cubed
2 t. dried parsley
1 t. onion powder
1 t. paprika
salt to taste
1 t. pepper
2 T. cornstarch

Place broth or water in a large stockpot over medium-high heat. Add
remaining ingredients except cornstarch; bring to a boil. Lower heat to
a simmer; cover and cook for about 1-1/2 hours. Shortly before serving,
place cornstarch in a small bowl. Add 1/4 cup cooking liquid; mix
well. Stir back into simmering stew; continue cooking for several
minutes, until thickened. Makes 4 to 6 servings.

Take advantage of the Christmas decorations that are
already filling stores in late autumn. Shiny gold glass balls
mix well with natural materials like pine cones for
an interesting contrast of textures...fill a tall glass
hurricane for a quick centerpiece.

152

A Bountiful Family Feast

Sweet Autumn Pork Chops

Jim Martineau
Delaware, OH

*I made up this recipe on a cool autumn night. It was an instant hit,
especially with our little daughter, Emily, who loves the mix of apples
and sweet potatoes. It's an often-requested fall dinner at our house.*

3/4 c. apple juice, divided
6 T. maple syrup, divided
4 boneless pork chops,
   3/4-inch thick
1-1/2 t. cinnamon, divided
1 t. garlic powder
1/2 t. pepper
1 T. olive oil

1 sweet potato, peeled and
   thinly sliced
1 sweet onion, thinly sliced
2 Bosc pears, cored and thinly
   sliced
1 Golden Delicious apple, cored
   and thinly sliced

Combine 1/2 cup apple juice and 1/4 cup maple syrup in a plastic
zipping bag. Add pork chops and turn to coat; refrigerate at least
2 hours. Mix one teaspoon cinnamon, garlic powder and pepper in a
cup. Remove pork chops from bag and dust with spice mixture; set
aside. Heat oil, 2 tablespoons apple juice and remaining maple syrup
in a large oven-safe skillet. Add vegetables and fruits; sprinkle with
remaining cinnamon. Sauté over medium heat for about 35 minutes,
stirring occasionally, until sweet potato is soft and mixture is
caramelized. Halfway through cooking time, add remaining apple
juice if mixture seems dry. Remove mixture from skillet; add pork
chops to skillet and top with mixture. Cover and bake at 400 degrees
for 35 minutes, or until pork chops are cooked through. Serves 4.

Dress up dining room chairs in a snap while directing guests
to their seats...tie a pretty ribbon around the chair back
and tuck in a folded placecard.

Nutty Sausage Dressing

Diane Chaney
Olathe, KS

No more ho-hum dressing...serve up this anything-but-bland mixture of cornbread, wild rice, sausage and walnuts.

1/2 c. butter
1 c. onion, chopped
2 c. celery, diced
3 carrots, peeled and shredded
4 c. sliced mushrooms
6-oz. pkg. long-grain and wild rice, cooked

16-oz. pkg. ground pork sausage, browned and drained
8-oz. pkg. cornbread stuffing mix
1 egg, beaten
1 c. chopped walnuts, toasted

Melt butter in a large skillet over medium heat; sauté onion, celery and carrots for 5 to 7 minutes, until crisp-tender. Add mushrooms; cook until tender and liquid has evaporated, about 10 minutes. In a large bowl, combine cooked rice, sausage and onion mixture. Stir in stuffing mix, egg and nuts; toss to mix well. Spoon into a greased 3-quart casserole dish. Bake, uncovered, for 40 to 50 minutes. May also be used to stuff a 16 to 20-pound turkey; roast as usual. Makes 12 to 14 servings.

Are you toting your Thanksgiving specialty over the river and through the woods? Make sure it arrives spill-free and piping hot. Wrap the baking dish in aluminum foil, then in several layers of newspaper before tucking it into an insulated container.

Granny's Apple Dressing

Geneva Rogers
Gillette, WY

Sometimes my grandmother would replace some of the almonds with sweetened dried cranberries for a festive touch. This dressing is scrumptious with roast turkey, chicken and pork.

1-1/2 c. onion, chopped
2 c. celery, sliced
1/2 c. butter
1-3/4 c. water
3 cubes chicken bouillon
12 c. dried bread cubes
3 c. tart apples, cored, peeled
   and coarsely chopped

Optional: 1 c. toasted slivered
   almonds
2 t. poultry seasoning
1 t. dried parsley
1/4 t. dried sage

In a skillet over medium heat, cook onion and celery in butter until tender. Add water and bouillon; cook until boiling and bouillon dissolves. Combine remaining ingredients in a large bowl; add onion mixture and mix well. Place in a greased 4-quart casserole dish. Bake, uncovered, at 350 degrees for 30 minutes, or until heated through. Makes about 2-1/2 quarts or 8 to 10 servings.

Start a Thanksgiving tradition! Lay a blank card on each dinner plate and invite guests to write down what they are most thankful for this year. Afterwards, bind the cards together with a ribbon to create a sweet gratitude book.

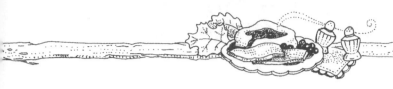

Yummy Beef Stroganoff

Katherine Murnane
Plattsburgh, NY

An oldie but goodie, loved by both family & friends.

2 T. butter, divided
2-1/2 lbs. beef round steak,
  cubed
1/4 c. all-purpose flour
6 onions, sliced
2 8-oz. cans whole mushrooms,
  drained

8-oz. can tomato sauce
1 cube beef bouillon
1 c. boiling water
1 c. sour cream
cooked rice or egg noodles

Melt one tablespoon butter in a large skillet over medium heat. Dredge beef in flour; sauté in butter until browned. Transfer beef to a greased 3-quart casserole dish. Add remaining butter to skillet and sauté onions; do not brown. Add mushrooms and sauce to casserole dish; dissolve bouillon cube in boiling water and stir to mix. Bake, covered, at 325 degrees for 1-1/2 to 2 hours. Just before serving, add sour cream and stir well. Serve over cooked rice or noodles. Serves 6 to 8.

If it's Thanksgiving now, Christmas can't be far away.
Why not double any festive must-have casseroles or
side dishes and freeze half for Christmas dinner...
you'll be so glad you did!

Connie's Meatloaf Roll

Connie Pritt
Coalton, WV

A local restaurant serves a meatloaf sandwich with roasted red peppers. I enjoyed it so much that I decided to try to recreate the meatloaf at home. The Swiss cheese is my special touch. I'm sure you'll love this meatloaf either as a main dish or on sandwiches!

2 lbs. ground beef
2 eggs, beaten
3/4 c. bread crumbs
1/4 c. catsup
1/4 c. milk
1/4 t. dried oregano

1/2 t. salt
1/4 t. pepper
6 slices Swiss cheese
7-oz. jar roasted red peppers,
   drained

Mix all ingredients except cheese and red peppers. Pat mixture into a 12-inch by 10-inch rectangle on aluminum foil. Arrange cheese slices, covering meatloaf. Place red peppers on top of cheese. Roll up meatloaf jelly-roll style and pinch edges together; place in an ungreased 13"x9" baking pan. Bake at 350 degrees for about one hour and 15 minutes. Makes 10 servings.

Children are sure to be helpful in the kitchen when they're wearing their very own kid-size aprons. Visit a craft store to select fabric crayons and plain canvas aprons, then let kids decorate their apron as they like. Follow package directions for making the design permanent.

Creamy Chicken Roll-Ups

Vickie

*I like to start this slow-cooker recipe on Saturday mornings.
After an afternoon of flea-marketing, I can just add a side of
steamed fresh asparagus for an easy meal.*

6 boneless, skinless chicken
   breasts, flattened
6 thin slices deli ham
6 slices Swiss cheese
1/4 c. all-purpose flour
1/4 c. grated Parmesan cheese
1/2 t. salt
1/4 t. pepper
2 T. olive oil
10-3/4 oz. can cream of chicken
   soup
1/2 c. white wine or chicken
   broth
cooked rice

Top each chicken breast with a slice of ham and a slice of Swiss cheese.
Roll up tightly; fasten with toothpicks. In a shallow bowl, mix flour,
Parmesan cheese, salt and pepper. Roll chicken in flour mixture; cover
and refrigerate for one hour. In a large skillet over medium heat, brown
chicken in oil on all sides. Arrange chicken in a slow cooker. Combine
soup and wine or broth; pour over chicken. Cover and cook on low for
4 to 5 hours, until chicken is cooked through. Serve chicken on cooked
rice, topped with some of the sauce from slow cooker. Serves 6.

Make it extra special for your family! Even if no guests are
coming for the holiday dinner, pull out the good china and
light some candles...you'll be making memories together.

A Bountiful Family Feast

Italian Potato Gâteau

Debby Storch
San Diego, CA

*Substitute diced salami for the ham, if you like...serve as either
a side dish or a light luncheon dish.*

8 potatoes, peeled, cubed and
   cooked
1/2 c. butter, divided
1/4 c. milk
salt to taste

2 eggs, beaten
8-oz. pkg. mozzarella cheese,
   cubed
1/4 lb. cooked ham, diced
1/4 c. dry bread crumbs

In a large bowl, mash cooked potatoes with 1/4 cup butter, milk and
salt to taste. Stir in eggs; mix in cheese and ham. Transfer to a lightly
greased 10"x7" baking pan. Sprinkle top with bread crumbs and dot
with remaining butter. Bake, uncovered, at 350 degrees for 10 to
15 minutes, until cheese is melted and top is lightly golden. Serves 8.

If you're traveling to join family for Thanksgiving,
make a trip bag for each of the kids...a special tote bag
or backpack that's filled with favorite small toys,
puzzles and other fun stuff, reserved just for road trips.
The miles will speed by much faster!

159

Homemade Turkey Pot Pie

Sarah Sullivan
Andrews, NC

Mmm...everybody's favorite after-Thanksgiving comfort food!

1/3 c. margarine
1/3 c. onion, chopped
1/3 c. all-purpose flour
1/2 t. salt
1/4 t. pepper
1-3/4 c. turkey broth

2/3 c. milk
2-1/2 to 3 c. cooked turkey, chopped
10-oz. pkg. frozen peas and carrots, thawed
2 9-inch pie crusts

Melt margarine in a large saucepan over low heat. Stir in onion, flour, salt and pepper. Cook, stirring constantly, until mixture is bubbly; remove from heat. Stir in broth and milk. Heat to boiling, stirring constantly. Boil and stir for one minute. Mix in turkey, peas and carrots; set aside. Roll out one pie crust and place into a 9"x9" baking pan. Pour turkey mixture into pan. Roll remaining crust into an 11-inch square; cut out vents with a small cookie cutter. Place crust over filling; turn edges under and crimp. Bake at 425 degrees for about 35 minutes, or until golden. Makes 4 to 6 servings.

Choosing a turkey? Allow about one pound per person plus a little extra for leftovers. For example, a 15-pound turkey would serve 12 people with enough left to enjoy turkey sandwiches, turkey tetrazzini or turkey soup afterwards.

A Bountiful Family Feast

One-Dish Chicken & Stuffing

Jeanne Allen
Menomonee Falls, WI

Serve with steamed, buttered broccoli for a complete meal that your family will love.

1-1/4 c. boiling water	paprika to taste
2 T. margarine	10-3/4 oz. can cream of
4 c. sage and onion stuffing mix	mushroom soup
4 to 6 boneless, skinless	1/3 c. milk
chicken breasts	1 T. fresh parsley, chopped

Stir together water and margarine until margarine melts. Pour over stuffing mix in a large bowl; toss lightly. Spoon stuffing mixture across the center of a lightly greased shallow 3-quart casserole dish. Arrange chicken on either side of stuffing. Sprinkle paprika over chicken. Mix soup, milk and parsley; spoon over chicken. Cover and bake at 400 degrees for 30 minutes, or until chicken is done. Serves 4 to 6.

When choosing candles for the dinner table, consider how well the scent will go with food. Natural beeswax candles have an appealing mild scent...their warm amber color enhances any harvest table too.

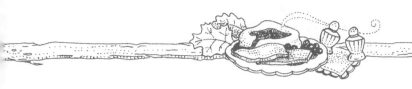

Yummy Veggie Bake

Linda Beaver
Irving, TX

This recipe will win over even veggie-haters! It's easy and fast to prepare too. This was a favorite for our cozy Wednesday night meals at my church, where I made some very close friends.

1/4 c. butter, divided
2 c. green beans, trimmed
1-1/2 c. carrots, peeled and cut
   into strips
3/4 c. green pepper, cut into
   1-inch pieces
1 onion, thinly sliced

2 c. celery, chopped
2 T. cornstarch
1 T. sugar
1/2 t. salt
2-1/2 t. pepper
14-1/2 oz. can diced tomatoes

Melt one tablespoon butter and spread in a 3-quart casserole dish. Layer fresh vegetables in dish. Combine cornstarch, sugar, salt and pepper; sprinkle over vegetables. Pour tomatoes with juice over top and dot with remaining butter. Cover and bake at 350 degrees for one hour, until vegetables are tender. Makes 8 to 10 servings.

Set mini white or orange pumpkins on top of tall candlesticks for a harvest centerpiece in a jiffy.

Warm Cinnamon Pineapple

Fran Fritz
Davenport, FL

Fresh pineapple...what a treat with a holiday baked ham!

1 whole pineapple
2 c. sugar

1/4 c. cinnamon

Slice off top and bottom of pineapple; gently slice off skin. Mix sugar and cinnamon in a shallow bowl. Roll pineapple in mixture until completely coated. Place on a large piece of aluminum foil; wrap tightly and set on a baking sheet. Bake at 350 degrees for 20 to 25 minutes, until warm throughout. Carefully unwrap pineapple; set upright onto a plate and slice vertically along sides, discarding core. Slice thinly and serve warm. Makes 10 to 12 servings.

Spiced Applesauce

Sheri Dulaney
Englewood, OH

Brown sugar and pumpkin pie spice makes this slow-cooker applesauce perfect for fall. Serve as a side dish or a simple dessert.

8 Golden Delicious Apples,
  cored, peeled and cubed
1/2 c. brown sugar, packed

1/2 c. water
1 t. pumpkin pie spice

Combine all ingredients in a slow cooker; stir to mix. Cover and cook on low setting for 8 to 10 hours, or on high setting for 3 to 4 hours. When done, stir with a wooden spoon. Gently crush applesauce against side of slow cooker to desired consistency. Makes 8 to 10 servings.

Add rosy red color and spicy flavor to homemade applesauce...just stir in a spoonful of red cinnamon candies as it's cooking.

Mom's Hominy & Cheese

Linda Walker
Erie, CO

This old-fashioned recipe came from my mother, who is no longer with us. She got it from the ladies of the Methodist church in Arvada, Colorado, where she worked for 25 years. I always think of her, and them when I make it. It is especially tasty with BBQ beef.

3 T. butter
1/4 c. onion, finely chopped
3 T. all-purpose flour
3/4 t. chili powder
1 t. salt
1/8 t. pepper

1-1/2 c. milk
2 15-oz. cans white hominy, drained and rinsed
8-oz. pkg. shredded Cheddar cheese

In a large saucepan over medium heat, melt butter and sauté onion until tender. Add flour and seasonings; cook and stir until bubbly. Slowly add milk; cook and stir until thickened. Stir in hominy; turn into a buttered 1-1/2 quart casserole dish. Top with cheese. Bake, uncovered, at 350 degrees for 35 to 40 minutes. Serves 6.

A fun holiday craft...hand turkey plates! Have kids trace around their hands with glass paint pens onto glass or ceramic plates. They can use their imagination to paint feathers, beaks and other details on their turkeys. Follow directions on the label for setting the paint permanently... you'll treasure these plates long after the children are grown.

Pecan-Butternut Squash Bake

Lisa Cameron
Twin Falls, ID

This recipe was first my Aunt Cheryl's and then my Grandma Bert's. Aunt Cheryl made it for one holiday dinner and once Grandma Bert tasted it, it became hers! Now it's a must at every family party or potluck...it is so good it could almost be a dessert.

1/3 c. butter, softened	1/4 t. cinnamon
3/4 c. sugar	1 t. vanilla extract
2 eggs, beaten	2 c. butternut squash, cooked
5-oz. can evaporated milk	and mashed

In a large bowl, blend together butter and sugar; beat in eggs, evaporated milk, cinnamon and vanilla. Add squash and mix well. Pour into a lightly greased 11"x 8" baking pan. Bake, uncovered, for 45 minutes, or until set. Sprinkle with Crunchy Topping and bake an additional 5 to 10 minutes. May be served hot or cold. Makes 4 to 6 servings.

Crunchy Topping:

1/2 c. crispy rice cereal	1/4 c. chopped pecans
1/4 c. sugar	2 T. butter, melted

Combine all ingredients; mix well.

Pumpkin pie spice is a blend of cinnamon, ginger, nutmeg and allspice, while poultry seasoning combines thyme, sage, marjoram, rosemary, pepper and nutmeg. Pick up a fresh can of each, early in the season...you'll be ready to spice up any sweet or savory dish.

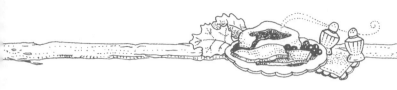

Tex-Mex Chicken Lasagna

Melody Taynor
Everett, WA

A hearty, zesty change from the usual casseroles...and it goes together in a jiffy! Dollop with sour cream or guacamole.

2 c. deli roast chicken, shredded
1 T. lime juice
1-1/2 t. chili powder
1 t. salt
1/2 t. pepper
1 onion, chopped
2 cloves garlic, chopped

1 T. oil
16-oz. jar salsa
15-oz. can chili with beans
4-oz. can chopped green chiles
9 6-inch flour tortillas
8-oz. pkg. shredded Mexican-
    blend cheese, divided

Toss chicken with lime juice and seasonings; set aside for 5 minutes. In a large skillet, sauté onion and garlic in oil for 3 to 4 minutes, until tender. Add salsa, chili and green chiles; reduce heat and simmer for 3 to 4 minutes. Line the bottom of a lightly greased 11"x7" baking pan with 3 tortillas. Layer with half of salsa mixture, half of chicken mixture and 1/3 of cheese. Repeat layers; top with remaining tortillas. Sprinkle remaining cheese on top. Bake, uncovered, at 350 degrees for 25 to 30 minutes. Let stand for 5 to 10 minutes before serving. Serves 6 to 8.

Do you have lots of leftover turkey? It freezes well up for to three months. Cut turkey into bite-size pieces, place in plastic freezer bags and pop in the freezer...ready to stir into hearty casseroles or soups later this winter when you'll enjoy it again.

Favorite Fall

Desserts

Mini Apple Dumplings

Valerie Harris
Valrico, FL

I found the idea for this recipe in a small cooking pamphlet over 25 years ago. I tweaked it to taste even better, and have made it every year at the first sign of cool weather. Every time I made it, my husband's and my three boys' faces would light up with glee. Now our daughters-in-law and our granddaughter Ivy love it too!

8-oz. tube refrigerated crescent
   rolls
1 Granny Smith apple, cored,
   peeled and sliced into
   8 wedges
8 caramels, unwrapped
2 to 3 t. butter, diced
1/4 c. sugar

1-1/2 T. cinnamon
Optional: 1/4 c. mini semi-sweet
   chocolate chips
1/4 c. powdered sugar
1 to 2 T. whipping cream or milk
Optional: 1/4 c. chopped
   walnuts

Separate crescent rolls and lay them on a lightly greased baking sheet. In the center of each triangle, place an apple slice, a caramel and 1/4 teaspoon butter. Mix sugar and cinnamon; sprinkle a small amount over rolls. If desired, sprinkle a few chocolate chips over each. Fold up all sides; pinch dough together to seal well. Fold to make a little pocket dumpling. Bake at 375 degrees for 11 to 13 minutes, until golden. In a small bowl, mix powdered sugar with enough cream or milk to make an icing that can be drizzled. Allow dumplings to cool slightly; drizzle with icing while still warm. Sprinkle with nuts, if desired. Serves 8.

For fall fun, grab your sweaters, pack a picnic lunch and take the family on a trip to an apple orchard. Pick your own apples, go on a wagon ride and sample fresh-pressed cider...what a sweet way to make memories!

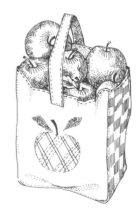

Taffy Apple Cupcakes

Angie Biggin
Lyons, IL

What fun...gooey caramel-topped cupcakes on a stick!

18-1/4 oz. pkg. carrot cake mix
1 c. Granny Smith apples, cored, peeled and finely chopped
1/2 t. cinnamon
20 caramels, unwrapped
1/4 c. milk
1 c. pecans or walnuts, finely chopped
12 wooden craft sticks

Prepare cake mix according to package instructions; stir in apples and cinnamon. Fill paper-lined jumbo muffin cups 2/3 full. Bake at 350 degrees for 20 to 25 minutes, until a toothpick inserted near center tests clean. Combine caramels and milk in a small saucepan over low heat; stir until melted and smooth. Spread caramel over cooled cupcakes; sprinkle nuts over top. Insert a craft stick into center of each cupcake. Makes one dozen.

Dress up plain paper napkins for dinner with a large turkey rubber stamp and a colorful stamp pad...oh-so festive!

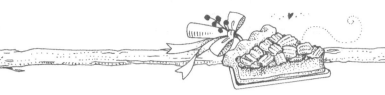

Chocolate Chip Cookie Cake

Ian White
Chesapeake, VA

My aunt shared this scrumptious recipe with me.

2-1/4 c. all-purpose flour
1 t. baking soda
1 t. salt
1 c. butter, softened
3/4 c. sugar

3/4 c. brown sugar, packed
1 t. vanilla extract
2 eggs, beaten
12-oz. pkg. semi-sweet
   chocolate chips

Combine flour, baking soda and salt in a medium bowl; set aside. In a separate large bowl, beat butter, sugars and vanilla until creamy. Add eggs, one at a time, beating well after each addition. Gradually beat in flour mixture. Stir in chocolate chips. Spread in a greased 16" round pizza pan. Bake at 350 degrees for about 20 minutes, until golden. Slice into wedges to serve. Makes 15 servings.

Freeze dollops of whipped cream ahead of time
to use for desserts...what a time-saver! Drop heaping
tablespoonfuls onto a chilled baking sheet and freeze.
Remove from the baking sheet and store in a plastic
zipping bag. At serving time, place a dollop on a
dessert portion...it will thaw in just a few minutes.

Favorite S'mores Pie

Lisa LaGaipa
Monroe, CT

My nieces just love s'mores, so I made this dessert for their high school graduation party...it was a huge hit! I hope you enjoy it as much as our family & friends do.

2/3 c. whipping cream
12 1-oz. sqs. semi-sweet
   baking chocolate
9-inch graham cracker crust
2-1/2 c. mini marshmallows,
   divided

1/4 c. milk
8-oz. container frozen whipped
   topping, thawed
Optional: chocolate curls

Pour cream into a microwave-safe medium bowl. Microwave on high for 1-1/2 minutes, or until very warm. Add chocolate squares; let stand for 2 minutes in microwave. Whisk until chocolate is melted and very smooth; pour into pie crust. Refrigerate for 30 minutes, or until firm. Combine 2 cups marshmallows and milk in a large microwave-safe bowl. Microwave on high for 1-1/2 minutes; stir until smooth. Refrigerate for 15 minutes, or until mixture is completely cooled. Stir in whipped topping; spread over chocolate mixture in crust. Refrigerate for at least 3 hours. Sprinkle remaining marshmallows on top. If desired, garnish with chocolate curls. Makes 8 servings.

Host a neighborhood pie party! Invite everyone to tie on an apron and bring their best-loved pie to share, along with extra copies of the recipe. Bring home some new-to-you recipes...one of them just might become a favorite!

Chocolate Pistachio Dessert

*Dawn Psik
Aliquippa, PA*

*This dessert is sooo light, creamy and tasty! It can be made well ahead
of time and refrigerated, so it's perfect for parties.*

3 c. milk
3.4-oz. pkg. instant pistachio
　pudding mix
3.4-oz. instant white chocolate
　pudding mix
8-oz. container frozen whipped
　topping, thawed

14.4-oz. pkg. graham crackers,
　divided
16-oz. container chocolate
　frosting

In a large bowl, whisk together milk and pudding mixes for 2 minutes.
Let stand for 2 minutes, until softly set. Fold in whipped topping. In
an ungreased 13"x9" baking pan, layer 1/3 of the graham crackers
and half the pudding mixture; repeat layers. Top with remaining
graham crackers. Refrigerate for at least one hour. Spoon frosting into
a microwave-safe bowl. Cover and microwave on high for 15 to
20 seconds until softened, stirring once. Spread over dessert. Chill for
at least 20 minutes, or until frosting is set. Makes 15 to 20 servings.

Winter is on the way...get ready by
making some super-easy fire-starters to
fill a basket by the hearth. Fold sheets
of newspaper into small squares and tie
package-style with kitchen string. To
use, tuck a square under the firewood
and light with a match.

Meringue Nut Pie

Corinne Britt
White Settlement, TX

This pie is really delicious and doesn't taste like a diet pie! I made up this recipe because my husband loved a special pie they served at a Luby's restaurant, but he and I are diabetic and I would not let him have it. This pie turned out so yummy that even our visitors do not suspect there's anything different about it.

1 c. chopped pecans or walnuts
1 c. saltine crackers, coarsely
   crushed
2 t. baking powder
4 egg whites, beaten
1/4 t. cream of tartar
1/2 c. sugar
1 t. vanilla extract

1-oz. pkg. sugar-free instant
   chocolate pudding mix
2-1/2 c. milk, divided
1.3-oz. env. whipped topping
   mix
Optional: 2 T. finely chopped
   pecans or walnuts

Mix together nuts, cracker crumbs and baking powder; set aside. With an electric mixer on low speed, beat egg whites until frothy. Increase speed to medium; add cream of tartar and beat until soft peaks form. Gradually beat in sugar. Beat on high speed until stiff peaks form; beat in vanilla. Fold in nut mixture with a spoon. Spread in a 9" pie plate that has been sprayed with non-stick vegetable spray. Place on middle rack of oven; bake at 325 degrees for 40 minutes. Let cool completely; crust may crack and fall slightly as it cools. Cover and refrigerate until ready to serve. Combine pudding mix and 2 cups milk; whisk together for 2 minutes. Let stand until softly set; pour into crust and smooth out. Combine topping mix and remaining milk; beat until stiff peaks form. Spoon over filling. If desired, sprinkle with nuts. Keep refrigerated. Makes 8 servings.

Small drawstring bags sewn of calico fabric are sweet table favors. Fill them with spiced tea bags for a special surprise.

Boiled Cider Spice Cake

Jeanette Busby
Dedham, MA

A delicious Bundt® cake...dust it with powdered sugar and give it the place of honor on the dessert table at Thanksgiving.

1 c. raisins
2 c. all-purpose flour, divided
1 c. apple cider
1 c. brown sugar, packed
1/2 c. butter
1/2 t. salt

2 t. baking powder
1 t. baking soda
1 t. cinnamon
1/2 t. ground ginger
1/2 t. nutmeg

Toss raisins in one tablespoon flour to coat. In a large pot, combine cider, brown sugar, butter and raisins. Bring to a boil over medium heat; remove from heat. Sift together remaining flour and all other ingredients. Add flour mixture all at once to hot mixture; immediately stir rapidly into hot mixture. Pour batter into a greased Bundt® pan. Bake at 350 degrees for about 30 minutes, or until firm and a toothpick tests clean. Cool cake in pan on a wire rack for 10 minutes. Turn cake out of pan and cool completely on rack; remove to a cake plate. Makes 8 to 10 servings.

Garnish a Bundt® cake with a sparkling bunch of sugared grapes...so pretty! Just brush grapes with a thin mixture of meringue powder and water, roll in fine sugar and let dry.

Tried & True Pecan Pie

Gloria Robertson
Midland, TX

In a word...delectable!

4 eggs
1 c. sugar
16-oz. bottle light corn syrup
1/2 c. butter, melted
1 t. vanilla extract

1/4 t. salt
3 c. pecan halves
Optional: 1 c. sweetened flaked
  coconut
2 9-inch deep-dish pie crusts

In a large bowl, beat eggs until frothy; whisk in sugar. Add corn syrup and mix well; mix in melted butter, vanilla and salt. Add pecans and coconut, if using; mix with a wooden spoon. Pour into crusts; bake at 400 degrees for 10 minutes. Reduce oven temperature to 350 degrees. Bake an additional 55 to 60 minutes, until a knife tip inserted in center comes out clean. Cool on wire racks. Makes 2 pies, 6 to 8 servings each.

For a crisp, golden top crust on pies, brush water over the unbaked crust and sprinkle it with sugar before popping into the oven.

175

Spicy Pumpkin Raisin Cake

Kimberly Pfleiderer
Galion, OH

An easy-to-make cake that's filled with fall flavors! Tuck a square into family members' lunchboxes for a sweet surprise.

2 c. all-purpose flour
2 t. baking powder
1 t. baking soda
1/4 t. salt
1 t. cinnamon
1 t. nutmeg
1 t. pumpkin pie spice
1/2 t. ground cloves

2 c. sugar
4 eggs, beaten
1 c. oil
15-oz. can pumpkin
1 c. raisins
16-oz. container cream cheese
    frosting

In a large bowl, combine all ingredients except frosting. Mix completely. Pour into a greased 13"x9" baking pan. Bake at 350 degrees for 40 to 50 minutes, or until a toothpick inserted in center comes out clean. Cool cake before frosting. Makes 10 to 12 servings.

Most fruit pies and cobblers can be frozen for as long as 4 months...what a time-saver! Cool completely after baking, then wrap well in plastic wrap and two layers of aluminum foil before freezing. To serve, thaw overnight in the refrigerator, bring to room temperature and rewarm in the oven.

Carrot Surprise Cake

Barbara Bower
Orrville, OH

This delicious recipe was shared with me by an old friend I worked with, years ago...it has been a family favorite for three generations now. Sometimes I use mini Bundt® pans too...just remember to decrease the baking time.

8-oz. pkg. cream cheese,
  softened
2 c. sugar, divided
4 eggs, divided
2 c. all-purpose flour
2 t. baking soda
2 t. cinnamon

1 c. oil
3 c. carrots, peeled and
  shredded
Optional: 1/2 to 1 c. chopped
  nuts, 1 c. golden or dark
  raisins
Garnish: powdered sugar

Blend together cream cheese, 1/4 cup sugar and one egg until well mixed; set aside. In a separate large bowl, combine remaining sugar, flour, baking soda and cinnamon. Add oil and remaining eggs; stir until moistened. Fold in carrots; add nuts or raisins, if desired. Reserve 2 cups of batter. Pour batter into a greased Bundt® pan. Spoon cream cheese mixture over batter and spread around pan. Spoon reserved batter over cream cheese layer. Bake at 350 degrees for 45 minutes, or until a toothpick tests clean. Let cake cool in pan for 10 minutes before turning out. Sprinkle with powdered sugar. Makes 8 to 10 servings.

Offer mini portions of rich cake, cobbler or pie layered in small glasses with whipped topping and a crunchy topping. Guests can take "just a taste" of something sweet after a big dinner or sample several yummy treats.

Praline Ice Cream Dessert

Emma Wilson
Cordell, OK

This is really yummy and hard to resist! It's handy to take to church socials or serve for Sunday dinner dessert...just make it ahead and pop it into the freezer.

2 c. all-purpose flour
1/2 c. quick-cooking oats, uncooked
1/2 c. brown sugar, packed
1 c. margarine, melted

1 c. chopped nuts
12-oz. jar caramel ice cream topping, divided
1/2 gal. vanilla ice cream, softened

Mix together flour, oats, brown sugar, margarine and nuts. Spread mixture on a lightly greased baking sheet. Bake at 400 degrees for 15 minutes, watching carefully to avoid burning. Let cool; crumble. Spread half of mixture in a greased 13"x9" baking pan. Drizzle with half of caramel topping; spread ice cream over topping. Sprinkle remaining crumbled mixture on top of ice cream. Drizzle with remaining topping. Freeze for 2 hours to overnight before serving. Makes 12 to 15 servings.

What we're really talking about is a wonderful day set aside on the fourth Thursday of November when no one diets. I mean, why else would they call it Thanksgiving?

-Erma Bombeck

Pumpkin Custard Crunch

Donna Borton
Columbus, OH

*I have made this festive dessert for years. I love pumpkin and make
a lot of oatmeal desserts, and just came up with the combination.
Try it plain or top it with vanilla ice cream like my husband does!*

29-oz. can pumpkin
3 eggs, beaten
2 t. pumpkin pie spice
1 t. cinnamon

14-oz. can sweetened
   condensed milk
1 c. milk
2 t. vanilla extract

Mix pumpkin, eggs and spices well; stir in condensed milk, milk and
vanilla. Pour into a greased 13"x9" baking pan; spoon Crunch Topping
over pumpkin mixture. Bake at 350 degrees for 45 to 60 minutes,
until a knife comes out clean. Watch carefully so that topping doesn't
burn. Serve warm. Makes 9 to 12 servings.

Crunch Topping:

3 c. quick-cooking oats,
   uncooked
1 c. brown sugar, packed
1 c. all-purpose flour

1 t. cinnamon
1 c. walnuts or pecans, crushed
1 c. margarine, melted

Stir together oats, brown sugar, flour, cinnamon
and nuts. Pour melted margarine over top;
toss to mix.

Kids will feel extra-special when
served sparkling cider or cranberry
juice cocktail in long-stemmed
plastic glasses.

179

Cinnamon-Apple Bread Pudding

Susan Fracker
New Concord, OH

My husband LOVES bread pudding but I am not a raisin fan.
This recipe is the result of a delicious compromise.

1 loaf cinnamon swirl bread,
  cubed
2 c. milk
4 eggs, beaten
1 c. applesauce
1 c. sugar

2 T. vanilla extract
1/2 t. cinnamon
1/4 t. nutmeg
1/4 c. butter, melted and cooled
  slightly

Place bread cubes in a large bowl and pour in milk; let stand a few
minutes until moistened. In a separate bowl, combine eggs, applesauce,
sugar, vanilla and spices. Drizzle melted butter over bread mixture;
toss lightly. Add egg mixture to bread mixture and stir well. Let stand
for 10 minutes. Place mixture in a buttered 13"x9" baking pan. Bake at
350 degrees for about 45 minutes, until golden and a knife tip inserted
in center comes out clean. Let cool slightly while making Caramel
Sauce. Serve warm, topped with sauce. Makes 10 to 12 servings.

Caramel Sauce:

18-oz. container caramel apple
  dip

1/4 c. half-and-half

Place caramel apple dip with half-and-half in a small saucepan. Cook
and stir over low heat until warm and smooth. Add a little more
half-and-half if too thick.

Enjoy a homestyle dessert like warm gingerbread or bread
pudding in front of a crackling fireplace...pure comfort!

Brenda's Fruit Crisp

Brenda Smith
Gooseberry Patch

Here's my favorite dessert recipe...it's a yummy way to use a bumper crop of peaches, apples or berries!

5 c. frozen peaches, apples or berries, thawed and juices reserved
2 to 4 T. sugar
1/2 c. long-cooking oats, uncooked
1/2 c. brown sugar, packed
1/4 c. all-purpose flour

1/4 t. nutmeg
1/4 t. cinnamon
1/4 t. vanilla extract
Optional: 1/4 c. sweetened flaked coconut
1/4 c. butter, diced
Optional: vanilla ice cream

Place fruit and juices in an ungreased 2-quart casserole dish; stir in sugar and set aside. In a medium bowl, mix oats, brown sugar, flour, spices, vanilla and coconut, if using. Add butter to oat mixture; combine until mixture becomes coarse. Sprinkle over fruit. Bake at 375 degrees until golden and tender, 30 to 35 minutes. Serve warm, topped with ice cream if desired. Serves 6.

Replace the graham cracker crust in your favorite pie recipe with a snappy new flavor! Crush gingersnap cookies to make one cup crumbs. Toss crumbs with 3 tablespoons melted butter, press into a pie plate and add filling as usual.

Country Pineapple Pie

Dianne Amyett
Granbury, TX

This was my grandmother's recipe. I can picture her puttering around in her little kitchen, with fresh black-eyed peas cooking in a pot, cornbread browning in an old cast-iron skillet and this delicious pineapple pie baking in the oven. What wonderful memories!

1/2 c. sugar
1/4 t. salt
1/4 c. cornstarch
1/3 c. water

20-oz. can crushed pineapple, drained and 1 cup juice reserved
2 9-inch pie crusts

Mix together sugar, salt and cornstarch in a small saucepan; add water and reserved pineapple juice. Cook over medium heat, stirring constantly until thick and clear. Add pineapple; remove from heat. Place one pie crust in a 9" pie plate; pour pineapple filling into crust. Add top crust; pinch to seal and cut vents. Bake at 425 degrees for 30 minutes. Makes 8 servings.

For a fresh table decoration, arrange berry-covered twigs of bittersweet in quart-size Mason jars. Fill jars with water. Set an oyster jar votive holder inside each jar rim and top with a votive candle.

Great-Grandma's Blue Goose Pie

Judy Taylor
Butler, MO

My mother-in-law is a fabulous cook and her kitchen table has been a haven of comfort for many years. After raising five children, she hasn't slowed down...if anything, she's become busier! Her children, grandchildren and now great-grandchildren are treated often to her tasty homemade cooking like this yummy berry pie.

2 9-inch pie crusts
2-1/2 to 3 c. sugar, divided
3 c. gooseberries

1 c. blueberries
3 T. instant tapioca
Garnish: water, 2 t. sugar

Place one pie crust in a 9" pie plate; sprinkle with 2 tablespoons sugar and set aside. Mix together berries and remaining sugar in a microwave-safe bowl. Microwave on high setting for about 5 minutes, checking often, until berries start to pop open. Transfer berry mixture to pie crust. Cover with top crust; crimp to seal and cut small slits in crust. Sprinkle crust with a little water and then sprinkle with sugar. Bake at 350 degrees until golden, about 45 minutes. Serves 5 to 6.

Need a few more chairs for the dining room table?
Mix-and-match tag-sale chairs are easily pulled together...
just add a coat or two of matching paint.

183

Caramel Flan Cheesecake

Julie Bruce
Simi Valley, CA

My husband loves flan, so I created this recipe for him. It's a delicious treat, especially when strawberries are in season...the combination is beyond decadent. My family & friends request it again & again for celebrations of all kinds.

16-oz. jar caramel ice cream
   topping
8-oz. pkg. cream cheese,
   softened
5 eggs
14-oz. can sweetened
   condensed milk

12-oz. can evaporated milk
1 t. vanilla extract
Garnish: whipped cream, extra
   caramel topping
Optional: strawberries, sliced
   and tossed with sugar

Remove lid from topping jar; microwave jar for about 15 seconds, until topping is pourable. Pour 1/3 cup topping into a 10" glass pie plate, tilting to coat bottom and sides. In a large bowl, beat cream cheese until smooth. Beat in eggs, one at a time. Beat in milks and vanilla until smooth; pour into pie plate and set aside. Place a wire rack in a roasting pan. Set pie plate on rack; place roasting pan in oven. Pour enough water into roasting pan to reach halfway up sides of pie plate. Bake at 350 degrees for 50 to 60 minutes, until center is just set. Cool for one hour on a wire rack; chill in refrigerator for 8 hours to overnight. To unmold, set pie plate in a shallow hot water bath for 5 minutes. Run a knife around edges of plate; invert onto a serving platter. Serve with whipped cream, extra topping and sliced strawberries, if desired. Makes 8 to 10 servings.

A bountiful garland for the mantel...tie ears of Indian corn, evenly spaced, onto a length of jute.

Favorite Fall *Desserts*

Ooey-Gooey Baked Apples

Lora Montgomery
Delaware, OH

Warm and cozy...yum!

6 Gala or Jonagold apples, cored
1/4 c. butter, softened
1/4 c. brown sugar, packed
1/4 c. maple syrup
1 t. cinnamon

1/2 c. raisins
1/2 c. walnuts, finely chopped
Garnish: 16-oz. jar caramel
   ice cream topping

Arrange cored apples in a lightly greased 13"x9" baking pan and set aside. Combine butter, brown sugar, maple syrup and cinnamon in a small bowl; stir in raisins and walnuts. Spoon mixture into center of apples; cover with aluminum foil. Bake at 325 degrees for one hour to one hour and 15 minutes, until apples are tender. Serve warm with caramel topping. Makes 6 servings.

When buying fresh baking spices, don't discard the old ones...use them in a stovetop potpourri. Add cinnamon sticks and whole cloves to a saucepan of water...toss in apple or orange peels too. Bring to a low simmer, adding more water as needed...delightful!

185

Halloween Cookie Pizza

Flo Burtnett
Gage, OK

Fun for kids to make...more fun to eat!

3/4 c. brown sugar, packed
1/2 c. shortening
1 egg, beaten
1 T. water
1 t. vanilla extract
1-1/4 c. all-purpose flour

1/2 t. baking soda
1/4 t. salt
1 c. butterscotch chips
1 c. mini marshmallows
1/2 c. milk chocolate chips
1/2 c. mixed nuts, chopped

Beat together brown sugar and shortening until light and fluffy. Add egg, water and vanilla; beat well. In a separate bowl, stir together flour, baking soda and salt; add to sugar mixture. Beat with an electric mixer on low speed until well blended. Stir in butterscotch chips. Spread batter in a lightly greased 12" round pizza pan, leaving a 1/2-inch border. Bake at 350 degrees for 11 to 13 minutes, until set. Remove from oven; sprinkle with marshmallows, chips and nuts. Bake for an additional 5 to 7 minutes, until marshmallows are golden. Cool completely. Drizzle with Chocolate and Orange Drizzles. Let stand until set, about one hour. Cut into wedges. Makes 16 to 20 servings.

Chocolate Drizzle:

1/4 c. milk chocolate chips   1-1/2 t. shortening

Place ingredients in a microwave-safe bowl. Microwave at 50% setting for one minute; stir. Continue microwaving for 15 seconds at a time, stirring each time until smooth.

Orange Drizzle:

1/2 c. powdered sugar   2 drops red food coloring
3 drops yellow food coloring   1 T. water

In a small bowl, stir together all ingredients. Stir until well blended.

Candy Bar Cake

Brandi Begley
Smyrna, TN

As a busy mom, I love this easy-to-make recipe! It's a clever way to use up mini chocolate candy bars left over from Halloween. It's my husband's favorite sweet treat too. I've made it several times for his company potlucks and everyone seems to love it. If you wish, use caramel ice cream topping in place of the chocolate syrup.

18-1/4 oz. pkg. chocolate
  cake mix
14-oz. can sweetened
  condensed milk, divided
16-oz. can chocolate syrup,
  divided

12-oz. container frozen whipped
  topping, thawed
10 to 12 fun-size candy bars,
  coarsely chopped

Prepare cake mix according to package directions; bake in an 11"x9" baking pan. Cool for about 30 minutes. With a fork, carefully poke through to the bottom, all over top of cake. Pour 3/4 of condensed milk over top, reserving remainder for another recipe. Let stand for 15 minutes. Pour 3/4 of chocolate syrup over milk. Cover and refrigerate overnight to allow milk and syrup to absorb completely. Frost cake with whipped topping; sprinkle with chopped candy bars. Drizzle with remaining chocolate syrup. Makes 12 servings.

Press whole cloves into the surface of a pillar candle to form a pattern...just right for a dessert buffet!

187

Butterscotch Dumplings

Lisa Knaus
Garnett, KS

This simple dessert uses everyday pantry ingredients, yet it is very sweet, delicious and filling. It has been a favorite of mine since I was little.

1 c. brown sugar, packed
1 T. butter
2 c. water
1-1/4 c. all-purpose flour
1 T. sugar

2 t. baking powder
1/4 t. salt
1/4 c. shortening
2/3 c. milk

Combine brown sugar, butter and water in a skillet; bring to a boil over medium heat. In a separate bowl, blend together flour, sugar, baking powder and salt. Cut in shortening until crumbly. Add milk; stir just until moistened. Drop batter by tablespoonfuls into boiling brown sugar mixture. Cover and cook over low heat for 15 minutes. Serves 6 to 8.

Make a tray of cute pumpkin cupcakes for a Halloween bake sale. Frost cupcakes with orange-tinted frosting and a sprinkle of orange sanding sugar. Top each cupcake with a small green gumdrop for a stem. So clever!

Pumpkin Bread Pudding

Cindy Pepper
Georgetown, DE

*A sweet change from the same ol' pumpkin pie! Garnish with
dollops of whipped topping and a dash of nutmeg.*

1 loaf white bread, torn into
    bite-size pieces
30-oz. can pumpkin pie filling
14-oz. can sweetened
    condensed milk

12-oz. can evaporated milk
4 eggs, beaten
1 c. milk

Place bread pieces in a greased 13"x9" glass baking pan; set aside.
In a separate bowl, combine pumpkin pie filling, condensed milk,
evaporated milk and eggs. Pour mixture over bread; stir until all
pieces are moistened. Add milk a little at a time; stir until well blended
and mixture is very moist. Bake at 350 degrees for 45 minutes. Serve
warm. Makes 12 servings.

Ask Grandma to spend an afternoon showing you
how to make the delicious dessert she's always been famous
for! Be sure to have a pad & pen handy to write down
every step, and a camera to take some snapshots.
Afterwards, you can sample it together along
with cups of steamy hot tea or coffee.

Choco-Mallow Cake

Dawn Raskiewicz
Alliance, NE

This is my own creation...it's a big hit with my husband too!

12-oz. pkg. marshmallows, divided

18-1/4 oz. pkg. yellow cake mix
12-oz. pkg. dark chocolate chips

Place half the marshmallows in a 13"x9" baking pan that has been sprayed with non-stick vegetable spray; set aside. Reserve remaining marshmallows for another recipe. Prepare cake mix according to package directions. Pour batter over marshmallows in the pan. Sprinkle chocolate chips over top of batter. Bake at 350 degrees for 32 to 37 minutes. Marshmallows will rise to top of cake and chocolate chips will sink to bottom. Makes 8 servings.

The frost is on the pumpkin! For an elegant yet easy fall centerpiece, spray a pumpkin lightly with spray adhesive and sprinkle with clear glitter. Set the pumpkin on a cake stand and cover with a clear glass dome.

Chocolate Zucchini Cupcakes

*Michelle Rooney
Sunbury, OH*

*These are so moist and delicious...no one will guess
the secret ingredient is zucchini!*

2 c. zucchini, shredded
3 eggs, beaten
2 c. sugar
3/4 c. oil
2 t. vanilla extract
2 c. all-purpose flour

2/3 c. baking cocoa
1/2 t. baking powder
1 t. baking soda
1 t. salt
3/4 c. milk chocolate chips

Stir together zucchini, eggs, sugar, oil and vanilla in a large bowl. Add flour, cocoa, baking powder, baking soda and salt; stir in chocolate chips. Spoon batter into 24 paper-lined muffin cups. Bake at 325 degrees for 25 minutes, or until a toothpick inserted near center comes out clean. Cool in pan on wire racks for 5 minutes. Remove from pan; cool completely. Frost with Peanut Butter Frosting. Makes 2 dozen.

Peanut Butter Frosting:

1/2 c. creamy peanut butter
1/3 c. butter, softened
1 T. milk

1/2 t. vanilla extract
1-1/2 c. powdered sugar

With an electric mixer on medium speed, beat peanut butter, butter, milk and vanilla until smooth. Gradually beat in powdered sugar. If necessary, stir in a little more milk until desired consistency.

A quick & easy harvest decoration for frosted cupcakes!
Flatten red, yellow and orange fruit roll-ups and cut
with a leaf-shaped cookie cutter, then press
the "leaves" onto cupcakes.

Aunt Helen's Apple Cake

Maryann Brett
Johnstown, PA

*I can remember eating this dessert at my Aunt Helen's house when
I was a very small girl. It was a real treat, like a pie and cake together
in one dessert. She passed away when I was very young, but every fall
I make this wonderful cake and remember my Aunt Helen. This is also
delicious for breakfast...if it lasts that long!*

2/3 c. shortening
1 to 1-1/3 c. sugar, divided
3 to 3-1/2 c. all-purpose flour
1-1/2 t. baking powder
2/3 t. salt
2/3 c. ice water

5 to 6 cooking apples, cored,
   peeled and thinly sliced
2 t. cinnamon
2 T. butter, diced
Garnish: milk
Optional: sugar, cinnamon

Mix shortening, 1/2 cup sugar, flour, baking powder, salt and water
until dough forms. Divide into 2 balls; roll out one ball to fit into
bottom and sides of an ungreased 8"x8" baking pan. Add enough
apple slices to fill pan almost to the top. Sprinkle apples with remaining
sugar to taste and cinnamon; dot with butter. Roll out remaining dough
to fit top of pan; press to edges of pan. Pierce dough with a fork to
vent. Brush with a small amount of milk. If desired, sprinkle with a
little sugar and cinnamon. Bake at 350 degrees for 50 to 60 minutes,
until crust is golden. Makes 9 servings.

Tuck a jar of homemade pie filling, a favorite pie recipe and
a pie bird into a pretty basket for a thoughtful hostess gift.

Treats & Sweets to Share

Brown Sugar-Apple Cookies

Nancy Hannon
Lewistown, PA

Perfect for sharing with friends over a steamy pot of spiced tea.

1 c. brown sugar, packed
2 eggs, beaten
1/2 t. baking soda
1 t. cinnamon
1/2 t. salt

1/2 c. shortening
2 t. vanilla extract
2 c. all-purpose flour
1 c. apples, cored, peeled
  and sliced

Mix all ingredients together, stirring in apples last. Drop by teaspoonfuls onto ungreased baking sheets. Bake at 350 degrees for 8 to 10 minutes. Makes 3-1/2 to 4 dozen.

Dress up a holiday table with leaf-printed placemats. Brush acrylic craft paint over the back of a leaf and press onto a large piece of paper. Repeat with more leaves to create a border or overall design. When dry, protect the placemat with clear self-stick plastic.

Butterscotch Spice Cookies

Kristy Markners
Fort Mill, SC

These are the easiest cookies to make...my two-year-old son loves them!

18-oz. pkg. spice cake mix
2 eggs, beaten
1/2 c. applesauce
1 T. vanilla extract

Optional: 1 c. long-cooking oats,
    uncooked
11-oz. pkg. butterscotch chips

Combine dry cake mix, eggs, applesauce and vanilla in a large bowl.
Add oats, if using. Beat with an electric mixer on low speed until well
blended. Stir in butterscotch chips. Drop by rounded teaspoonfuls,
2 inches apart, on parchment paper-lined baking sheets. Bake at
375 degrees for 8 to 10 minutes, until set. Cool cookies for 2 minutes
on baking sheets. Remove to wire racks to finish cooling. Makes
about 3 dozen.

Invite friends over for an old-fashioned candy-making party!
Pull taffy or stir up some chocolate fudge...you'll have
a sweet time together.

Quick Crescent Pecan Pie Bars

Tonya Lewis
Scottsburg, IN

I love pecan pie, but these bars are super-quick & easy to make.

8-oz. tube refrigerated crescent
   rolls
1/2 c. sugar
1/2 c. corn syrup

1 T. butter, melted
1/2 t. vanilla extract
1 egg, beaten
1/2 c. chopped pecans

Unroll dough into 2 long rectangles; place in an ungreased
13"x9" baking pan. Press over bottom and 1/2-inch up sides of pan
to form a crust. Press perforations firmly to seal. Bake at 375 degrees
for 5 minutes; remove from oven. In a medium bowl, combine
remaining ingredients; mix well. Pour over partially baked crust.
Bake an additional 18 to 22 minutes, or until golden. Cool and cut
into bars. Makes 2 dozen.

Toss together a yummy snack mix in a jiffy! Mix equal
amounts of sweetened dried cranberries, salted peanuts
and chocolate chips...great for munching on a
leaf-peeping hike or at get-togethers.

Treats & Sweets to Share

Chocolate Oat Drops

Marilyn Roberts
Alamo, TN

Everyone's favorite no-bake cookies! I used to make them when I was a child, I made them for my children and I make them now for my grandchildren. They never last more than a day!

2 c. sugar
1/3 c. baking cocoa
1/2 c. milk
1/2 c. margarine, softened
3 c. quick-cooking oats,
    uncooked

1/2 c. plus 1 T. crunchy peanut
    butter
1 t. vanilla extract

In a Dutch oven, mix together sugar and cocoa; add milk and margarine. Cook over medium heat, stirring frequently, to a full rolling boil. Let boil without stirring for one minute and 15 seconds. Remove from heat. Add oats and peanut butter; stir until well blended. Add vanilla and mix well. Quickly drop by tablespoonfuls onto wax paper. Let stand until set. Store in an airtight container. Makes 2 dozen.

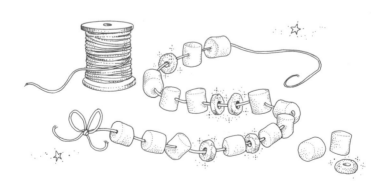

Set little ones down with a bowl of fruit-flavored cereal rings and a piece of dental floss...they can make cereal necklaces (and nibble away!) while you're baking.

Sweet Kiss Clusters

Sharon Davenport
Eldon, MO

These nutty, fudgy candies are a favorite at all our family holiday get-togethers...snack days at work too!

7-oz. jar marshmallow creme
12-oz. pkg. chocolate drops
2-1/2 c. sugar

5-oz. can evaporated milk
1/4 c. butter, sliced
2 c. pecan halves

Place marshmallow creme and chocolate drops in a large heatproof bowl; set aside. Combine sugar, evaporated milk and butter in a saucepan over medium heat. Bring to a boil; cook for 8 minutes. Pour over mixture in bowl; stir well until chocolate melts and is well blended. Stir in pecans. Drop by teaspoonfuls onto wax paper; let stand until set. Makes 6 dozen.

Sending home sweet treats with guests? For a fun and easy container, pick up a shiny new paint can from the home-improvement store to decorate with scrapbooking paper or even vintage wallpaper.

Honey-Glazed Snack Mix

Karolyn Skubal
Ainsworth, IA

My kids' favorite after-school snack...it's scrumptious to carry along on fall outings too. You may even want to double the recipe.

5 c. bite-size crispy corn cereal
   squares
1 c. mini pretzel twists

1 c. pecan halves
1/3 c. margarine
1/4 c. honey

In a large bowl, combine cereal, pretzels and pecans; toss to mix and set aside. Melt margarine and honey together in a small saucepan over low heat; blend well. Pour over cereal mixture; stir to coat evenly. Spread in a 15"x10" jelly-roll pan that has been sprayed with non-stick vegetable spray. Bake at 350 degrees for 12 to 15 minutes, or until mixture is lightly glazed, stirring halfway through. Let cool slightly; spread on wax paper to cool completely. Store in an airtight container. Makes about 7 cups.

A jug of cider with a mulling spice bag makes a thoughtful hostess gift. For 2 quarts cider, place one teaspoon each of cloves, allspice and orange zest into a small muslin drawstring bag. Tie it to a 2-quart jug of cider along with 2 to 3 cinnamon sticks and a note that says: "Simmer spices in cider until hot and bubbly...enjoy!"

Cute Turkey Cookies

Flo Burtnett
Gage, OK

*On Thanksgiving morning, let the kids keep busy
making this fun recipe/craft to set at everyone's place.*

40 fudge-striped cookies,
   divided
1/4 c. chocolate frosting

2 5-oz. pkgs. chocolate-covered
   cherries
20 pieces candy corn

Place 20 cookies on a flat surface, chocolate-side down, for the base. With frosting, attach a cherry to the top of each base cookie. Position another cookie perpendicular to each base cookie; attach with frosting. With a dab of frosting, attach one piece of candy corn to the front of each cherry for the head. Let stand until set. Makes 20.

Fill a tall apothecary jar with old-fashioned rock candy sticks in bright fall colors to use as hot beverage stirrers.

Spiced Pumpkin Bars

Becky Riedesel
Sioux City, IA

I haven't met anyone yet who doesn't love these dessert bars!
I actually prefer them to pumpkin pie during the holidays. The
recipe came from my Mothers of Preschoolers (MOPS) group.

3 eggs, beaten
15-oz. can pumpkin
1 c. sugar
12-oz. can evaporated milk
1 t. vanilla extract
1 t. cinnamon

1/2 t. ground ginger
1/4 t. ground cloves
18-oz. pkg. spice cake mix
3/4 c. butter, thinly sliced
1 c. chopped pecans

In a large bowl, beat eggs and pumpkin together. Blend in sugar, evaporated milk, vanilla and spices. Pour into a greased 13"x9" baking pan. Sprinkle dry cake mix evenly over top of batter. Dot with butter slices, making sure to place some in corners of pan. Sprinkle pecans over top. Bake at 350 degrees for 55 minutes. Cool; cut into bars. Makes 12 to 16 servings.

A whimsical Halloween centerpiece that can double as take-home favors. Insert 12-inch dowels into the bottom of mini pumpkins. Paint on Jack-'O-Lantern faces, tie on ribbon streamers and stand in a tall vase.

Double-Dark Chocolate Brownies

Terri Lotz-Ganley
South Euclid, OH

My grandson just loves these...they are the only dessert he asks for!
They are so moist they don't need any frosting.

1-1/2 c. butter, melted
3 c. sugar
2 t. chocolate or vanilla extract
2 t. almond extract
6 eggs, beaten

1-1/2 c. all-purpose flour
1 c. baking cocoa
1-1/2 t. baking powder
1-1/2 t. salt
1 c. semi-sweet chocolate chips

Combine melted butter, sugar and extracts in a large bowl; mix well.
Add eggs and beat well with spoon. In a separate bowl, mix flour,
cocoa, baking powder and salt. Gradually add flour mixture to butter
mixture; beat until well blended. Add chocolate chips and stir well.
Spread batter evenly in a 13"x9" glass baking pan that has been
sprayed with non-stick vegetable spray. Bake at 350 degrees for
30 to 40 minutes, until a toothpick inserted in the center tests clean.
Cool on a wire rack; cut into bars. Makes about 1-1/2 dozen.

Dress up a dessert tray in no time for a festive ending
to your party! Place homemade treats in shiny gold
or silver paper muffin liners.

202

Mocha Chocolate Cookies

Sheila Murray
Tehachapi, CA

These are the best cookies! My family loves them...
you can't just eat one!

12-oz. pkg. semi-sweet
  chocolate chips, divided
2 T. instant coffee granules
2 t. boiling water
1-1/4 c. all-purpose flour
3/4 t. baking soda

1/2 t. salt
1/2 c. butter, softened
1/2 c. sugar
1/2 c. brown sugar, packed
1 egg, beaten
1/2 c. chopped walnuts

Place 1/2 cup chocolate chips in a small microwave-safe bowl; microwave for 30 seconds to one minute, until melted. Stir until smooth; cool to room temperature. In a small cup, dissolve instant coffee in boiling water; set aside. In a separate small bowl, combine flour, baking soda and salt; set aside. In a large bowl, combine butter, sugars and coffee mixture; beat until creamy. Add egg and melted chocolate; mix well. Gradually add flour mixture. Stir in remaining chocolate chips and nuts. Drop by rounded tablespoonfuls onto ungreased baking sheets. Bake at 350 degrees for 10 to 12 minutes. Allow to stand for 2 to 3 minutes before removing from baking sheets. Makes about 3 dozen.

Tuck a cookie into a glassine envelope and tie on a tag
stamped, "Thanks...for all you do!" Make up a batch
to hand out to the mail carrier, the babysitter,
the dog groomer, the bus driver and all those other
oh-so-helpful folks we just don't remember to thank
as often as we should.

Allison's Cake Balls

Sharon Mull
McKinney, TX

*God bless my daughter-in-law, Allison. She is the reason that I first started buying **Gooseberry Patch** cookbooks many years ago...the first one I purchased was for one of her wedding shower gifts! She shared this recipe with me after one of her Book Club parties. The flavor variations are endless!*

18-1/4 oz. favorite-flavor
   cake mix
16-oz. container favorite-flavor
   frosting, divided

20-oz. pkg. dark or white
   melting chocolate, chopped

Prepare cake mix according to package directions; bake in a
13"x 9" baking pan. Let cake cool. Turn cake into a large bowl and
crumble into small pieces. Add half of frosting; mix well. Roll mixture
into one-inch balls; refrigerate for about an hour. Place chocolate in a
microwave-safe container. Microwave on high for 60 seconds. Stir;
continue cooking on high for another 30 seconds, or until completely
melted. Stir until smooth. Dip balls into melted chocolate with a fork
or a candy dipping tool; place on wax paper-lined baking sheets. Place
in refrigerator again for about 10 minutes, until chocolate sets. Store
in an airtight container. Makes 4 dozen.

Delight dinner guests with a tiny ribbon-tied box
at each place setting...inside they'll find a piece of
scrumptious homemade fudge.

204

Luscious Chocolate Truffles

Cherylann Smith
Efland, NC

I give these decadent candies as gifts to my friends. They're inexpensive, but oh-so good. I pack them in tins with a mixture of other goodies.

6-oz. pkg. semi-sweet chocolate
  chips
1/2 c. cream cheese, softened
1-1/2 c. powdered sugar
1/2 t. vanilla extract
1 t. favorite-flavor extract

Garnish: baking cocoa,
powdered sugar, flaked
coconut, chopped nuts,
candy sprinkles or additional
melted chocolate

Place chocolate chips in a microwave-safe container. Microwave on high for 60 seconds. Stir; continue cooking on high for another 30 seconds, or until completely melted. Let cool slightly. In a separate large bowl, beat cream cheese until smooth. Add powdered sugar and continue beating until well blended. Stir in melted chocolate and extracts. Refrigerate for 2 hours, or until firm. Form into one-inch balls. Roll balls in desired garnish or dip in melted chocolate. Cover; keep refrigerated. Makes 3 dozen.

Are you toting chocolate truffles to a get-together?
Nestle them in an egg carton...they'll arrive
looking as scrumptious as they started.

Zucchini Drop Cookies

Kathleen Sturm
Corona, CA

My Aunt Laina shared this recipe with me. We love these spicy cookies, which are filled with raisins and walnuts as well as shredded zucchini. A tasty way to use up a garden surplus!

1/2 c. margarine, softened
1 egg, beaten
1 c. sugar
2 c. all-purpose flour
1 t. baking soda
1/2 t. salt

1 t. cinnamon
1/2 t. ground cloves
1 c. zucchini, shredded
1 c. raisins
1 c. chopped walnuts

In a large bowl, blend together margarine, egg and sugar; set aside. In a small bowl, combine flour, baking soda, salt and spices. Add to margarine mixture; mix well. Stir in zucchini, raisins and walnuts. Cover and refrigerate for one to 2 hours. Drop by tablespoonfuls onto greased baking sheets. Bake at 350 degrees for 12 to 15 minutes. Makes about 2 dozen.

Turn faceted glass candy dishes into sparkly candles... just fill with sweet-scented wax chips and add a wick. Group together on a mirrored tray for extra sparkle.

Iced Carrot Cookies

Paula Purcell
Plymouth Meeting, PA

When my now 29-year-old married daughter was a toddler, one of her favorite stories was called "Rabbit Finds a Way," about a bunny who just loved cakes and cookies made with carrots. Erin wanted to make these cookies whenever we read the story!

1 c. butter, softened	2 c. all-purpose flour
3/4 c. sugar	2 t. baking powder
1 egg, beaten	1/2 t. salt
1 c. carrot, peeled, cooked and mashed	1 t. vanilla extract
	3 to 4 drops almond extract

Blend together butter and sugar; add egg and carrots. In a separate bowl, sift flour, baking powder and salt together; add to butter mixture, blending well. Stir in extracts. Drop by teaspoonfuls onto greased baking sheets. Bake at 375 degrees for 10 minutes, or until just lightly golden. Test for doneness with a toothpick. Frost cooled cookies with Powdered Sugar Frosting and let dry. Makes 3 dozen.

Powdered Sugar Frosting:

1/4 c. butter, softened	3 T. orange or lemon juice
2 c. powdered sugar	1 T. orange or lemon zest

Blend butter and powdered sugar. Add juice and zest; mix well.

Wrap baked goods in sheets of wax tissue paper before tucking into a gift box...it comes in pretty seasonal prints and will preserve their freshness.

Maple Popcorn Balls

Marjorie Wilser
Goleta, CA

*This is my friend Elizabeth's recipe. Be sure to have a helper handy
to help shape the balls before the popcorn mixture cools!*

24 c. popped popcorn
2 c. golden raisins
2 c. chopped nuts
2/3 c. maple syrup
1-1/2 t. maple extract

2/3 c. apple juice
1/2 c. butter, sliced
3/4 t. salt
2 c. sugar

Combine popcorn, raisins and nuts in a large bowl. Mix remaining
ingredients in a large heavy saucepan. Cook and stir over medium
heat until sugar dissolves. If mixture tries to rise above pan, lower
heat. Watch closely, as temperature will rise very quickly toward the
end. Stop stirring just before mixture reaches hard-crack stage, or
290 to 310 degrees on a candy thermometer. Immediately remove
from heat and pour over popcorn mixture; stir to coat. Working
quickly with buttered hands, form into tennis ball-sized balls. Cool;
wrap in cellophane. Makes about a dozen.

Butterscotch Bits

Becky Havens
Lake Ridge, VA

Once you've had a taste, you can't stop eating them!

11-oz. pkg. butterscotch chips
1 c. creamy peanut butter

8 c. corn & rice cereal
1 c. milk chocolate chips

In a large saucepan over low heat, melt butterscotch chips and peanut
butter, stirring frequently. Fold in cereal until pieces are coated. Fold in
chocolate chips just until combined, but not melted. Spread on a wax
paper-lined baking sheet; chill until set. Break into pieces; store in an
airtight container. Makes 16 servings.

Treats & Sweets to Share

Mom's Peanut Butter Candy

Patricia Woolsey
Hanover, MI

Back in the early 1950's, my mother would make this candy for the fall festivals when I was in elementary school. It was always one of the first treats to sell out, and I remember I was always so proud of her. It's really very simple and makes a nice presentation.

1 c. creamy peanut butter   1 T. half-and-half
1 c. powdered sugar   24 pecan halves

Combine peanut butter and powdered sugar in a medium bowl. Add half-and-half and combine with hands until well mixed. Form into a ball. Roll out to a log one-inch in diameter, 24 inches long. Cut into bite-size pieces; press a pecan half onto each piece. Makes 2 dozen.

Still have fun-size chocolate candy bars left over from Halloween? Use them to make deluxe s'mores...yummy!

209

Nanny's Shortbread Chews

Paula McFadden
Owensboro, KY

My Aunt Nanny always had a batch of these cookies waiting for me whenever I came for a visit. I have her handwritten recipe framed in my kitchen, as she passed on a few years ago.

1/2 c. butter, softened
1-1/2 c. brown sugar, packed
   and divided
1 c. plus 2 T. all-purpose flour,
   divided
2 eggs, beaten

1 t. vanilla extract
1 t. baking powder
1/2 t. salt
1 c. chopped walnuts or pecans
1-1/2 c. chopped dates or
   raisins

In a medium bowl, mix butter, 1/2 cup brown sugar and one cup flour together until the consistency of fine crumbs. Press into the bottom of a greased 13"x9" baking pan. Bake at 350 degrees for 8 to 10 minutes; remove from oven. Mix remaining brown sugar and flour, eggs, vanilla, baking powder and salt; blend well. Stir in nuts and dates or raisins; pour mixture over baked crust. Return to oven; bake an additional 15 to 20 minutes. Cool; cut into squares. Makes 2 dozen.

Cats, bats and other spooky Halloween cut-out cookies call for lots of black frosting. Here's a handy hint...start with chocolate frosting and you'll only need to add a small amount of black food coloring.

Spicy Maple-Anise Snaps

Judy Gillham
Whittier, CA

This old-fashioned German icebox cookie is a much-requested family favorite. It even won me a ribbon at the Los Angeles County Fair! I've been perfecting it over the years and have found this delicious blending of anise and maple that really pleases.

1 c. butter, softened
1 c. sugar
1 c. dark brown sugar, packed
1 egg, beaten
1 t. maple extract
2-1/2 c. all-purpose flour

1 t. baking soda
1 t. cinnamon
3/4 t. ground cloves
1 T. anise seed, ground
1/2 c. pecans, finely chopped

In a large bowl, blend together butter and sugars until fluffy. Beat in egg and extract; set aside. In a separate bowl, combine remaining ingredients except pecans; mix well. Gradually blend flour mixture into butter mixture; add pecans and mix in well. Divide dough into 3 parts; form each into a log, 8 inches long. Wrap tightly in wax paper; refrigerate about an hour, until very firm. Remove one roll at a time from refrigerator and slice 1/4-inch thick. Place on parchment paper-lined baking sheets, one to 2 inches apart. Bake at 375 degrees for 10 to 12 minutes, until golden. Immediately remove cookies from baking sheets; cool completely on wire racks. Store tightly covered in airtight containers. Flavor of cookies will develop over the next day or so. Makes 7 dozen.

Crispy Chocolate Chippers

Jenna Fowls
Warsaw, OH

This was my great-grandmother's recipe. She gave it to her daughter, my grandma, and she gave it to me. I love having a recipe that has been in the family for so many years!

2-1/2 c. all-purpose flour
1 t. baking soda
1/2 t. salt
1 c. butter, softened
3/4 c. sugar
3/4 c. brown sugar, packed

2 eggs, beaten
1 t. vanilla extract
2 c. crispy rice cereal
6-oz. pkg. semi-sweet chocolate
 chips

Sift flour, baking soda and salt together; set aside. In a separate large bowl, combine butter and sugars; blend well. Add eggs and vanilla; beat well. Add flour mixture; blend well. Stir in cereal and chocolate chips. Drop by tablespoonfuls onto greased baking sheets. Bake at 350 for about 10 minutes, until lightly golden. Cool cookies on baking sheets for one minute; remove from sheets and cool on wire racks. Makes 6 dozen.

Scoop up sweet autumn-themed vintage postcards at tag sales and turn a plain jar candle into an extra-special gift in minutes! Just color copy the postcard, secure it to the front of a jar candle with spray adhesive and it's done.

Crunchy Cashew Mix

Denise Faust
LaFontaine, IN

Mmm...this sweet snacking mix is irresistible!

9 c. crispy corn or rice cereal
   squares
9-oz. can cashews
2 c. sweetened flaked coconut
1/2 c. butter

1/2 c. corn syrup
1 c. brown sugar, packed
1 t. vanilla extract
1/2 t. baking soda

Combine cereal, cashews and coconut in a large heat-proof bowl; set aside. Melt butter in a large saucepan over medium heat; add corn syrup and brown sugar. Stir well and bring to a boil; boil for 5 minutes. Remove from heat; stir in vanilla and baking soda. Pour over cereal mixture; stir well to coat. Pour mixture out onto a greased 15"x10" jelly-roll pan. Bake at 250 degrees for one hour, stirring every 15 minutes. Store in an airtight container. Makes about 25 servings.

Here's a quick trick if you're serving up snack mix or popcorn to a crowd. Use coffee filters as disposable bowls... afterwards, just toss 'em away!

Pumpkin Whoopie Pies

Vickie

Everyone loves these big, soft marshmallow-filled sandwich cookies!

1 c. canned pumpkin
1/3 c. butter, softened
18-1/2 oz. pkg. spice cake mix

2 eggs, beaten
1/2 c. milk

With an electric mixer on medium speed, beat pumpkin and butter together until smooth. Add dry cake mix, eggs and milk. Beat on low speed until combined; increase speed to medium speed and beat for one minute. Drop by heaping tablespoonfuls, 3 inches apart, onto parchment paper-lined baking sheets. Bake at 375 degrees for about 15 minutes, until set and edges are lightly golden. Carefully remove cookies to a wire rack; cool. Spread half of cookies with 2-1/2 tablespoons filling; top with remaining cookies. Keep chilled. Makes 15.

Marshmallow Filling:

8-oz. pkg. cream cheese, softened
1/2 c. butter, softened
1-1/2 c. marshmallow creme

1 t. vanilla extract
1/2 t. cinnamon
1/2 t. nutmeg
2 c. powdered sugar

Blend together cream cheese and butter until smooth. Add remaining ingredients; beat until well combined.

Congo Squares

Susan Slattery
Liberty Township, OH

This recipe belongs to my grandmother...it has been a family favorite for decades. I don't know how these yummy chocolate bites got their name, but I do know that they're so good they never last long around our house!

16-oz. pkg. brown sugar
2/3 c. butter, melted
3 eggs, beaten
2-2/3 c. all-purpose flour

2-1/2 t. baking powder
1/2 t. salt
1 c. semi-sweet chocolate chips
1 c. chopped walnuts

Blend brown sugar, butter and eggs in a large bowl. Sift flour, baking powder and salt into brown sugar mixture; stir well. Add chocolate chips and nuts; mix well. Spread evenly in a greased 13"x9" baking pan. Bake at 350 degrees for about 30 minutes, until lightly golden and set in center. Cool; cut into squares. Makes 3 dozen.

If the grandparents live out of town, why not invite an older neighbor or friend of the family to join you and the kids in a cookie baking day? You're sure to have fun together.

Beth's Caramel Corn

Beth Hershey
Denver, PA

One year I made this sweet, crunchy popcorn treat as gifts
for my family...they all loved it!

16 c. popped popcorn
1 c. butter
1-2/3 c. brown sugar, packed
1/2 c. corn syrup

1 t. salt
1/2 t. baking soda
1 t. vanilla extract

Spray a roasting pan with non-stick vegetable spray. Place popcorn in pan; set aside. Melt butter in a large heavy saucepan over medium heat; stir in brown sugar, corn syrup and salt. Bring to a boil, stirring constantly. Stop stirring; continue to boil for exactly 5 minutes. Remove from heat; stir in baking soda and vanilla. Gradually pour hot mixture over popcorn; mix well. Cover and bake at 250 degrees for one hour, stirring every 15 minutes. Spread on parchment paper until completely cooled. Break apart; store in an airtight container. Makes about 12 servings.

On Halloween the thing you must do
Is pretend that nothing can frighten you.
And if something scares you
and you want to run,
Just let on like it's Halloween fun!

-19th-century postcard verse

Caramel Marshmallow Treats

Shirley McGlin
Black Creek, WI

Turn these scrumptious tidbits into party pops! Use lollipop sticks instead of toothpicks and add some candy sprinkles to the cereal mixture.

14-oz. pkg. caramels,
   unwrapped
14-oz. can sweetened
   condensed milk

1 t. vanilla extract
16-oz. pkg. marshmallows
13-1/2 oz. pkg. crispy rice
   cereal

Place caramels, condensed milk and vanilla in a microwave-safe container. Microwave on high for about 2 to 3 minutes, until melted; stir until blended. With a toothpick, roll marshmallows in caramel mixture; roll in cereal to coat. Set on a buttered plate to cool. Makes about 5 dozen.

Giving a gift card for a birthday or other special occasion?
Make it memorable...slip the card into a festive take-out
container alongside some cello-wrapped homemade cookies.
Tie curling ribbons to the handle...how sweet!

217

Pistachio Thumbprints

Shawna Green
Dumas, TX

My good friend, Lisa, is an awesome cook and shared this recipe with me. Everyone raves about these delicious cookies!

1 c. margarine, softened
1/3 c. powdered sugar
1 egg, beaten
1 t. vanilla extract
3/4 t. almond extract
2 c. all-purpose flour

3.4-oz. pkg. instant pistachio
  pudding mix
1 c. pecans, finely chopped
1/2 c. semi-sweet chocolate
  chips
2 t. shortening, melted

In a large bowl, blend together margarine, powdered sugar, egg and extracts. Stir in flour and dry pudding mix. Form dough into one-inch balls; roll in pecans. Place on greased baking sheets; gently press a thumbprint into each ball. Bake at 350 degrees for 10 to 12 minutes. Cool cookies. Place a teaspoon of Vanilla Filling in each thumbprint. Combine chocolate chips and shortening in a plastic zipping bag. Microwave on high until melted, about one to 2 minutes, stirring every 15 seconds. Snip off the tip of one corner; drizzle chocolate over cookies. Let stand until set. Makes 3 dozen.

Vanilla Filling:

2 T. margarine, softened
2 c. powdered sugar

1 t. vanilla extract
2 T. milk

Blend all ingredients together until smooth.

For a super-quick thumbprint cookie filling, simply top baked cookies with a chocolate drop while they're still warm.

218

Nana's Raisin Squares

Beth Donofrio
Nokomis, FL

My Nana brought Raisin Squares wherever she went: church bake sales, holiday dinners, babysitting sleepovers...there was no occasion that didn't deserve Raisin Squares. I had graduated college before I realized other people had never even heard of them! When she died, the only thing I asked for was this recipe, which was written in my grandfather's meticulous penmanship and kept in Nana's pell-mell cookbook. I made sure I made them the very next Christmas Eve when we all got together.

3 c. all-purpose flour
1-1/2 t. salt
3/4 c. shortening
1/2 c. ice water

2 T. butter, diced
juice of one lemon
Garnish: powdered sugar

Combine flour, salt, shortening and ice water. Mix well and form into 2 balls. Roll out each ball into a 15-inch by 10-inch rectangle. Place one dough rectangle on an ungreased 15"x10" jelly-roll pan; spread with Raisin Filling. Dot with butter; drizzle with lemon juice. Top with remaining dough rectangle; pierce with a fork. Bake at 350 degrees for one hour. Cool; cut into squares and sprinkle with powdered sugar. Makes 2 dozen.

Raisin Filling:

3 T. all-purpose flour
2-1/2 c. water
15-oz. pkg. raisins

1/2 c. sugar
1-1/2 t. cinnamon

Mix flour and water in a saucepan; add remaining ingredients. Stir over medium heat for 5 to 8 minutes. Set aside to cool.

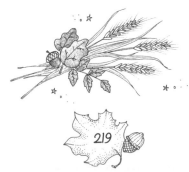

INDEX

Appetizers

Antipasto Crescent Bites, 42
Apple-Pecan Log, 22
Berry Good Kielbasa, 23
Beth's Party Piggies, 33
Boo's Pimento Cheese, 31
Charlie's Chicken-Chive Dip, 39
Cheddar Cheese Crispies, 29
Chicken Florentine Quesadillas, 25
Crabmeat-Stuffed Eggs, 43
Crispy Potato-Bacon Puffs, 32
Crunchy Cashew Mix, 213
Honey-Glazed Snack Mix, 199
Mari's Special Salsa, 37
Mexican Nacho Chips, 24
Mini Veggie Pizzas, 35
Pepperoni Pinwheels, 34
Pepperoni Pizza Dip, 20
Pizza Nibblers, 21
Snackin' Seeds, 45
Spicy Chili Crackers, 44
The Dip Lady's Famous Dip, 36
Too-Good-to-Stop Spread, 28
Yummy Campfire Cheese, 30
Zesty Pretzel Dip, 38

Beverages

Cadillac Cocoa, 46
Creamy Cocoa 3 Ways, 40
Hot Cranberry Punch, 27
Hot Vanilla, 41
Maple Cream Coffee Treat, 66
Spiced Apple Tea, 26

Breads

Auntie Rosie's Onion Bread, 92
Bacon Bread, 102
Bountiful Bread, 55
Broccoli Cornbread, 93
Chocolate Chip-Pumpkin Muffins, 61
Cranberry-Pumpkin Loaf, 54
Garlic Bubble Bread, 81
Lucille's Mexican Cornbread, 79

Breakfast

All-in-One Breakfast Bake, 58
Apple-Cinnamon Pancakes, 48
Autumn Sweet Potato Hash, 70
Baked Egg Soufflé, 57
Cheddar-Chile Brunch Potatoes, 59
Chicken & Waffles, 53
Cranberry Crescent Rolls, 51
Garden Quiche, 56
Garlic Mushrooms on Toast, 52
Hashbrown Breakfast Pizza, 63
Hashbrown Brunch Bake, 68
Kathy's Bacon Popovers, 62
Make-Ahead Sausage Brunch Bake, 62
Marsha's Breakfast Delight Scones, 60
Mom's Special French Toast, 57
New England Cider Doughnuts, 50
Potato & Onion Frittata, 65
Sausage & Jack Pie, 64
Smoked Salmon Strata, 69
Sweet & Spicy Bacon, 49

Cookies & Candies

Allison's Cake Balls, 204
Beth's Caramel Corn, 216
Brown Sugar Apple Cookies, 194
Butterscotch Bits, 208
Butterscotch Spice Cookies, 195
Caramel Marshmallow Treats, 217
Chocolate Oat Drops, 197
Congo Squares, 215
Crispy Chocolate Chippers, 212
Cute Turkey Cookies, 200
Double-Dark Chocolate Brownies, 202
Iced Carrot Cookies, 207
Luscious Chocolate Truffles, 205
Maple Popcorn Balls, 208
Mocha Chocolate Cookies, 203
Mom's Peanut Butter Candy, 209
Nana's Raisin Squares, 219
Nanny's Shortbread Chews, 210
Pistachio Thumbprints, 218
Pumpkin Whoopie Pies, 214

INDEX

Quick Crescent Pecan Pie Bars, 196
Spiced Pumpkin Bars, 201
Spicy Maple-Anise Snaps, 211
Sweet Kiss Clusters, 198
Zucchini Drop Cookies, 206

Desserts

Aunt Helen's Apple Cake, 192
Boiled Cider Spice Cake, 174
Brenda's Fruit Crisp, 181
Butterscotch Dumplings, 188
Candy Bar Cake, 187
Caramel Flan Cheesecake, 184
Caramel-Apple Bread Pudding, 67
Carrot Surprise Cake, 177
Choco-Mallow Cake, 190
Chocolate Chip Cookie Cake, 170
Chocolate Pistachio Dessert, 172
Chocolate Zucchini Cupcakes, 191
Cinnamon-Apple Bread Pudding, 180
Country Pineapple Pie, 182
Favorite S'mores Pie, 171
Great-Grandma's Blue Goose Pie, 183
Halloween Cookie Pizza, 186
Meringue Nut Pie, 173
Mini Apple Dumplings, 168
Ooey-Gooey Baked Apples, 185
Praline Ice Cream Dessert, 178
Pumpkin Bread Pudding, 189
Pumpkin Custard Crunch, 179
Spicy Pumpkin Raisin Cake, 176
Taffy Apple Cupcakes, 169
Tried & True Pecan Pie, 175

Mains

Anne's Chicken & Dried Beef, 137
Baked Spaghetti, 114
Brandi's Chicken & Artichokes, 112
Buttermilk Baked Chicken, 116
Caramelized Onion Pot Roast, 148
Connie's Meatloaf Roll, 157
Cowboy Dinner, 111
Creamed Chicken on Toast, 129
Creamy Chicken Roll-Ups, 158
Crunchy Chicken "Toes," 104
Dad's Best Mac & Cheese, 146

Dijon Roast Turkey, 134
Fiesta Chicken Casserole, 106
Fiesta Skillet Chicken, 119
Grandma's Spaghetti Casserole, 142
Hamburger Gravy & Potatoes, 122
Hearty Sauerkraut Platter, 149
Homemade Turkey Pot Pie, 160
Honey-Glazed Chicken, 150
One-Dish Chicken & Stuffing, 161
Party Ham Casserole, 110
Patti's Macaroni Casserole, 124
Perfect Cheesy Pasta Bake, 115
Pork Chops in Mushroom Sauce, 140
Pumpkin-Sausage Penne, 138
Quick Turkey Cordon Bleu, 118
Reuben Casserole, 132
Rolled Flank Steak, 144
Rosemary Pork Chops, 108
Savory Shrimp & Pasta Toss, 143
Speedy Shepherd's Pie, 120
Spuds & Sausages One-Dish, 121
Sweet Autumn Pork Chops, 153
Tex-Mex Chicken Lasagna, 166
Thankful Turkey Casserole, 105
Vermont Maple Chicken, 141
Yummy Beef Stroganoff, 156

Salads

Bountiful Apple Salad, 77
Cabbage Fruit Slaw, 76
Grandma's Pear Salad, 94
Jan's Redskin Potato Salad, 97
Minestrone Pasta Salad, 86
Mrs. Morris' Hot Chicken Salad, 125
Pineapple-Cranberry Salad, 95
Warm German Potato Salad, 96
Warm Orzo Salad, 87
Zesty Artichoke Salad, 80

Sides

Aunt Ruby's Sweet Potatoes, 127
Callie's Potato Casserole, 117
Creamy Broccoli Casserole, 130
Creamy Zucchini Bake, 113
Good-On-Anything Veggie Sauce, 131
Grandma's Buttery Mashed Potatoes, 135

INDEX

Sides (cont'd)

Granny's Apple Dressing, 155
Italian Potato Gâteau, 159
Janice's Cranberry Sauce, 139
Lori's Best Brussels Sprouts, 145
Mary's Sweet Corn Cake, 99
Mom's Hominy & Cheese, 164
My Three Veggies Dish, 126
Nutty Sausage Dressing, 154
Pecan-Butternut Squash Bake, 165
Queenie's Potato Deluxe, 109
Rich Turkey Gravy, 135
Roasted Asparagus & Squash, 139
Shoepeg Corn & Chiles, 107
Smothered Mushrooms, 128
Southern Hashbrown Casserole, 147
Spiced Applesauce, 163
Sweet Potato-Apple Bake, 151
Warm Cinnamon Pineapple, 163
Wild Rice & Mushrooms, 145
World-Famous Green Beans, 123
Yummy Veggie Bake, 162

Soups & Stews

Autumn Beef Barley Soup, 82
Beefy Nacho Cheese Soup, 78
Carolina Garden Stew, 152
Cheesy Broccoli Soup, 90
Classic French Onion Soup, 88
Easy Chicken Noodle Soup, 101
Easy Taco Soup, 98
Hearty Autumn Stew, 136
Hearty Vegetable-Beef Soup, 73
Hobo Stew, 84
Minnesota Wild Rice Soup, 74
Mom's Chilly-Day Cheese Soup, 89
Rose's Cream of Potato Soup, 91
Slow-Cooker Steak Chili, 100
Slow-Simmered Split Pea Soup, 75
The Great Pumpkin Chili, 85
Tom Turkey Noodle Soup, 83
Tortellini Sausage Soup, 72

homecoming parades colorful leaves

casual get-togethers

drives in the country

moonlit hayrides

craft fairs

crackling bonfires community suppers

U.S. to Canadian recipe equivalents

Volume Measurements

1/4 teaspoon	1 mL
1/2 teaspoon	2 mL
1 teaspoon	5 mL
1 tablespoon = 3 teaspoons	15 mL
2 tablespoons = 1 fluid ounce	30 mL
1/4 cup	60 mL
1/3 cup	75 mL
1/2 cup = 4 fluid ounces	125 mL
1 cup = 8 fluid ounces	250 mL
2 cups = 1 pint =16 fluid ounces	500 mL
4 cups = 1 quart	1 L

Weights

1 ounce	30 g
4 ounces	120 g
8 ounces	225 g
16 ounces = 1 pound	450 g

Oven Temperatures

300° F	150° C
325° F	160° C
350° F	180° C
375° F	190° C
400° F	200° C
450° F	230° C

Baking Pan Sizes

Square		Loaf	
8x8x2 inches	2 L = 20x20x5 cm	9x5x3 inches	2 L = 23x13x7 cm
9x9x2 inches	2.5 L = 23x23x5 cm	Round	
Rectangular		8x1-1/2 inches	1.2 L = 20x4 cm
13x9x2 inches	3.5 L = 33x23x5 cm	9x1-1/2 inches	1.5 L = 23x4 cm